LIFE IN A MEXICAN TOWN

Gerald W. Petersen

National Textbook Company
a division of NTC *Publishing Group* • Lincolnwood, Illinois USA

Acknowledgments
Photo on page 19 courtesy of American Airlines. All
other photos by the author.

Published by National Textbook Company, a division of NTC Publishing Group.
© 1992 by NTC Publishing Group, 4255 West Touhy Avenue,
Lincolnwood (Chicago), Illinois 60646-1975 U.S.A.
Manufactured in the United States of America.

1 2 3 4 5 6 7 8 9 ML 9 8 7 6 5 4 3 2 1

Preface

Altagracia is an imaginary town set in the southern part of the central plateau of Mexico. It is not meant to represent any one town. On the contrary, characteristics of several towns have been combined to form a typical town of that part of Mexico, the region known as the *bajío*. Immense differences of geography, climate, and culture make it impossible to represent all of Mexico.

Life in a Mexican Town introduces students to everyday life in Mexico. Every effort has been made to appeal to a broad range of age groups and interests, from high school to even junior college and college levels. This book can supplement a regular Spanish text. Many students find language learning more interesting and rewarding if they have a better understanding of the culture. Unfortunately, many texts have little cultural information. In addition, this book could be used profitably by teachers of history or geography who would like to introduce their students to the people and culture of Mexico.

The Classroom Activities at the back provide questions and activities that could be used in class or given as homework. There are exercises for individual or group work. Many of the activities could be used for oral reports, term papers, or group discussions.

There is no inherent logic in the sequence of chapters. Teachers should feel free to use the material in any order they wish. In a brief study like this one, it is impossible to delve deeply into the material presented. Teachers should feel free to enlarge on topics. Additional research will only enrich the material that is already there. Of course, students can also add new information by carrying out research or by reporting on their own travels or living experiences in Mexico.

The views and information presented are the author's, based on his research and experience in Mexico. Inevitably, other people will have other views or will have had other experiences. Teachers should not hesitate to add to examples or modify information with their own knowledge. Certainly there is no single correct view of a culture.

I would like to thank my wife, Jean, for her patience. I also am grateful to Jane and Jesús García, for the information and suggestions they have generously provided. Most of all I would like thank the Mexican people who with their warmth, friendship, and balanced lives have taught me so much.

G. W. P.

Contents

Introduction

Altagracia is located in the *bajío* or "lowland," of central Mexico. Although *bajío* means lowland, the plains here are between 5,500 and 7,000 feet in altitude and are low only in relation to the surrounding mountains. This lowland area includes the western part of the state of Querétaro, including the capital of the same name; the northern part of the state of Michoacán; much of the state of Guanajuato, including the cities of Celaya, Salamanca, and León; and the eastern part of the state of Jalisco. The size of this region is about 10,000 square miles. The Río Lerma and other rivers have made these plains a fertile region.

The surrounding mountains contain more than vegetation. In 1548 rich silver deposits were discovered near the city of Guanajuato, bringing in a rush of prospectors and miners. Later, rich mines were also developed in the Zacatecas and San Luis Potosí areas. All of these mining areas were located in the territory inhabited by the Chichimec Indians who fiercely resisted the Europeans' efforts to build up the region. Nevertheless, within a few years, a number of mines were operating. Thousands of miners, many of them Indians, performed the back-breaking work.

The mines proved to be fabulously profitable. To take the silver out and bring in supplies to the mining area, trading routes were established to Mexico City and from there east to Vera Cruz or west to Acapulco, the two major seaports. Spanish soldiers in *presidios* (forts) guarded the main road. To supply the mines with tools, equipment, and clothing, small industries sprang up in the small towns along the roads. Commercial agriculture developed to provide food for the thousands of miners. This combination of mining, agriculture, industry, and trade caused the towns to grow. Among the towns along this route was Altagracia.

Altagracia, located along the main route from Mexico City to the northern mining areas, became prosperous, since everything had to pass through it—the silver from the mines going south and the luxury items from Mexico City and Acapulco going north. Altagracia also had a textile mill which produced cotton (called *manta*) clothing, and blankets and an iron and steel industry that produced spurs, stirrups, knives, machetes, and pistols.

Because of this wealth, Altagracia developed the same complex social divisions found in Mexico City. At the top were the proud and arrogant *peninsulares*, Spaniards born in Spain. The most important positions in the government, the army, and the Church were reserved for them. Next came the *criollos*, people of European ancestry who were born in Mexico. They were the owners of the large agricultural holdings, the factories, and the mills. The *criollos* lived lives of wealth and splendor, building handsome, large homes and ornate churches. They enjoyed many diversions, feast days, and public celebrations. Below them were the *mestizos*, people of mixed Spanish and Indian blood. These were the farmers, the workers in the small manufacturing plants, the small shop owners, and the miners. At the bottom of the social ladder were the Indians. They were treated almost like slaves and were forced to carry out the most difficult and dangerous tasks requiring physical labor. The mestizos and Indians were deeply resentful of their poverty and lack of power. Even the *criollos* resented the fact that they were considered inferior to their Spanish parents or grandparents.

In the early 1800s, revolutionary ferment reached Altagracia. The American and French revolutions had set a precedent for armed struggle for freedom; books by thinkers of Europe's Enlightenment spread ideas of freedom and equality. The final push for revolt against the motherland came when Napoleon invaded Spain and placed his brother on the throne. Throughout the *bajío*, literary clubs met to discuss these events and to plot revolution. Among the leaders of these conspiracies were Ignacio Allende in the nearby town of San Miguel and Father Miguel Hidalgo in Dolores.

On September 16, 1810, Father Hidalgo rang the church bells in Dolores, gathered the poor mestizos and the Indians, and gave the first cry for independence in Mexico. Those listening to him took up whatever tools they could use as weapons and marched off on what would be a bloody eleven-year struggle for independence. In honor of their long struggle, the *bajío* is known as the Cradle of Independence, and the city of Dolores is now known as Dolores Hidalgo.

Today Altagracia is a town of 50,000 people. It is located on a hillside, overlooking a broad, green valley. From a distance it presents a picturesque sight. Dominating the view is the church tower. The domes of other churches also stand out among the reddish roof tiles, the chimneys, and the rooftop water tanks. Since there is ample rainfall in the *bajío* region, an abundance of vegetation fills the town. In the bottom of the valley, about five miles away, is a lake that is used for irrigation.

The climate in Altagracia is very pleasant. Because of its southern location, the winters are fairly mild. There is no snow, and seldom does it get cold enough for water to freeze. Due to its high altitude (6,000 ft.), the summers are also mild. Very rarely does the temperature reach 90° Fahrenheit. The average temperature ranges from a high of 68° in summer to a low of 57° in winter, a spread of only eleven degrees! The winters are dry, but the summers are accompanied by frequent heavy rainshowers. During the months of July and August, rain usually falls for more than 20 days each month.

The area surrounding Altagracia is predominantly an agricultural region. The main crops are corn, beans, and sorghum (used for cattle feed). There are also a few large cattle ranches and several large chicken farms.

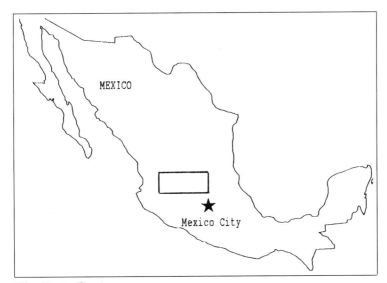

The Bajio Region

Map of Altagracia

Map Key

1. Main Church (Templo San José)
2. Theater (el Teatro Nervo)
3. Railroad Station (Estación FFNM)
4. Church (Iglesia Loreto)
5. Lookout (el Mirador)
6. State Offices (Oficinas del Estado)
7. Telephone Office (Central Telefónica)
8. Telegraph Co. (Oficinas de Telégrafos)
9. Post Office (Oficina de Correos)
10. Market (el Mercado)
11. Hospital (Centro Médico)
12. Library (la Biblioteca)
13. Police (la Comisarío de Policía)
14. Bus Station (Terminal de Autobuses)
15. Soccer Field (Cancha de Fútbol)
16. Education Center (Centro de Capacitatión)
17. Art School (Escuela de Arte)
18. Hotel del Virrey
19. Municipal Offices (la Presidencia Municipal)

♦♦♦ 1. ♦♦♦

The Town Layout

A. The Central Streets

The highway from Querétaro forks on the outskirts of the town to the east. One fork, the Calzada Santa Rosa (often called the *periférico*), bypasses the main part of town to the south. It joins the highway to San Miguel de Allende just west of the town. To the north of the fork, a smaller road leads to the Colonia Los Arcos, a poor residential area. Continuing straight ahead, the highway from Querétaro becomes Insurgentes, the main street. A six-to-eight-inch high and one-foot wide raised speed bump (*tope*) forces drivers to slow down as they approach the city's center. Other *topes*, which are jokingly called "sleeping policemen," are found throughout the town.

In the center of the city is the main square, the Plaza Allende, named for the hero of the Independence, Ignacio Allende. Insurgentes Street runs along the south side of the square. Though barely

A downtown street

1

A small side street

wide enough for two-way traffic, it is filled with cars, trucks, buses, bicycles, and motorcycles most of the day. During the busiest hours, police officers direct traffic on the corners of Aldama and Allende. Around the plaza, there is also heavy pedestrian traffic during much of the day.

Only Insurgentes Street is paved. The other downtown streets are cobbled. Most drivers carefully make their way along the rough surfaces of these streets, and pedestrians also must pay attention to where they place their feet.

Hidalgo Street runs along the northern end of the square. The Municipal Offices (*la Presidencia Municipal*), the State Offices (*las Oficinas del Estado*), and the Police Station (*la Comisaría de Policía*) all face the square on Hidalgo Street. The police in all of Mexico are divided into two branches: the Transit Police (*la Policía de Tránsito*), which handles all traffic and parking matters, and the *Comisaría de Policía*, which handles all other police matters. They are both located in the police station. The mayor, Alejandro Palacios, is called *el presidente*, or president, of the city. The largest park in the town, the "Parque Juárez," is four blocks to the east on Hidalgo. In the park there are peaceful walkways, several tennis courts, and a basketball court, in addition to a profusion of plants, flowers, and trees. The cemetery (*el Panteón*) is located five blocks west of the square on Hidalgo.

Allende Street runs along the east side of the square. Facing the square is the largest church in Altagracia, *el Templo San José*. The Bus Station (*Terminal de Autobuses*) is three blocks to the south on

Allende. The Telegraph Office (*Oficina de Telégrafos*) is found one block south of the square, while the Post Office (*Oficina de Correos*) is located one block to the north.

At most times of the day, street corners in the center of town are crowded with an array of vendors selling fruit, popcorn, shaved ices (*nieves*), vegetables, candy, and many assorted foods. In the evening, they set up tables and sell tacos and boiled ears of corn (*elotes*). Of course, many people like to sprinkle hot chili powder on their tacos and *elotes*. Under the north arcade of the plaza, protected from the rain, are more permanent sidewalk vendors. They sell candies (*dulces*), soft drinks (*refrescos*), newspapers (*diarios*), toys (*juguetes*), and trinkets.

One of these stands is owned and operated by Onofre Rosas and his wife Jesusa. They are proud that their business is prospering. Unlike some other vendors, they can afford to send their children to school. In the afternoons, their children Marcos and Anita join them to help out at the stand. When business is slow, the children sit in the shade of the arcade and do their homework.

On the opposite side of the square, *mariachis* gather in the evening in full dress, all waiting for employment to sing serenades or to sing for parties. Then there are the beggars (*mendigos*) who hold out their palm or a cup. These beggars may invoke the name of God when requesting money. Most people give them something, even if it's only a way to get rid of small coins. Also, there are a number of walking vendors who offer baskets, necklaces, tree bark paintings, strings of garlic (in season), and chewing gum (*chicle*). Car washers, with their buckets of water and some old rags, offer to wash cars. Bootblacks, carrying a small box on which clients place their foot, also look for business.

In these central streets the noise of passing cars mixes with that of the public buses, and the enticing aroma of food from many stores pervades the atmosphere with the smell of coffee, bread, fruits, and pastries. Among the most colorful of the characters who wander the central streets are the charlatans (*charlatanes*). These smooth-tongued salesmen have received their name because of their ability to attract a crowd with their oratory skills and to sell their wares. Their success is based more on their sales acumen and charm than on the merits of the product. These *charlatanes* offer the most incredible items—from all-purpose stain removers to small hand tools for cutting potatoes, apples, carrots, and other fruits in the shapes of flowers, spirals, butterflies, cubes, and tubes. Other products include creams, salves, and lotions for curing diseases; amulets for good luck; and disappearing ink. The *charlatán* is memorable not only for his gift of gab but also for his ability to make a living by his wits.

An impressive view of the town can be seen from the lookout to the northeast. The *mirador*, located at the top of Cuesta de San José Street, affords a view of the entire town nestled in the valley below. In the near distance lies the irrigation lake, then farmland stretches for miles beyond, and finally in the far distance, the Sierra de Guanajuato is visible. The *sierra* is the mountain range that overlooks the city of Guanajuato.

B. The Main Square

The main square is the heart of Altagracia. It was designed and constructed during the colonial period. Located in the center of the city, it is frequently called the *jardín* (garden) by the locals due to the abundance of trees and plants. The square is rectangular in shape and is bordered and crisscrossed by paths and streets which are lined with trees, bushes, and multicolored flowers. Spacious areas of grass separate the paths. White benches, distributed along the paths, provide a comfortable spot to rest in the shade and enjoy the surroundings.

In a large circular space in the center of the *jardín* stands the monument dedicated to Francisco Madero, a hero of the Mexican Revolution. A lovely pool of water, containing goldfish and coins, surrounds the monument. Little Marcos Rosas and his sister Anita often toss coins into the pool and solemnly make their wishes. Although his mother scolds him for wasting money, Marcos still believes that one day he'll toss in a magic coin and his wish will be granted. Of course,

The main square

A bootblack at work

he can't tell anyone his wish or it will never come true, but his father has a pretty good idea that a shiny new bicycle would probably make his son a believer in magic for all time.

In contrast to the magical pool, the principal institutions of Altagracia ring the *jardín*. Among them are the largest church, the Municipality, and the Courthouse (*Tribunal de Justicia*). In addition, some of the nicest shops and restaurants in Altagracia front the square. Some of the restaurants spill onto the sidewalk, under the arches which extend from the buildings to the street. The locals refer to these as *los arcos*.

The daily routine in the *jardín* seldom varies, except on holidays. In the early morning hours, people hurry through the square on their way to work. Delivery men bring supplies, such as ice, bread, vegetables, and meat, to the restaurants and shops around the square.

A youthful vendor

Templo de San José

Vendors and bootblacks begin to set up for the day, converting the square into their place of work. Among these street vendors and workers are the balloon, ice-cream, and peanut vendors, as well as the photographer with his three-legged camera, ready to produce an instant picture. As the morning progresses, older retired men come and sit on benches in the sunshine to read the newspaper or to talk with friends. Don Ramón López, now that he is older, leaves the garage in the care of his son and grandson and stops by the square to visit with old friends. Their topic of conversation usually centers on the situation in the country (*la situación del país*). They only stop talking to watch the maids and homemakers cross the square on their way to the shops and markets. During the day, mothers and maids bring children for a walk and to play. Children run through the open spaces as they play, filling the square with laughter and contentment.

At two in the afternoon, businesses, schools, and public buildings begin closing down for the two-hour lunch and siesta period. The *jardín* bustles and hums as workers, students, and public officials head home for the most important meal of the day. Then a stillness falls over the almost deserted square. At four in the afternoon, the *jardín* comes to life again as businesses and public offices reopen and

A child at play

students go to afternoon classes. Later in the afternoon, many people come to the square to walk or to sit and visit with friends. Entire families enjoy the occasion, and sweethearts stroll hand in hand. In Altagracia these happy scenes of conversation, friendship, and love continue until eight at night when the shops, markets, and public offices again close down, and everyone heads home for dinner (*la cena*).

On weekends, especially on Sundays, people of all ages crowd the *jardín*. Teenagers and young adults especially enjoy coming to the square on the weekends. They chat with friends who pull up in cars, buy refreshments from vendors, and stroll around the square. In fact, this is one of the main areas where young men and women meet one another and where dating and courtship take place.

C. Space and Distance

Mexicans are accustomed to a daily life of direct interaction with many people in the streets, on the buses, in cafés and restaurants, on

A group of teenagers

Afternoon in the square

the sidewalks, at work, and even at home. In their interactions they usually stand closer together than do people in English-speaking cultures. This difference often causes awkward moments and misunderstandings.

When a Mexican talks to a visitor from the U.S., the visitor often backs up to put more distance between himself and the Mexican to whom he is talking. The Mexican, however, moves forward in order to maintain the closer distance that is comfortable for him.

This Mexican town life of streets filled with people, heavy traffic, shouts of street vendors, and a great variety of shops brings an abundance of sensory experiences. The sights, sounds, and odors everywhere constantly affect the lives of the people. This sensory richness can be seen in the way they eat, speak, write, or receive a guest. In general this means less space between people in social situations and much ornamentation and color in their speech and in their signatures (*la rúbrica*). All of this reveals their personality. Everyday conversation involves using many hand and facial gestures, touching each other on the arms or shoulders, hand-shaking, pats on the back, and among women, a kiss on the cheek when saying goodbye.

Because total space needs must be maintained in balance, urban Mexicans have learned to make the most of parks and the outdoors. To León Suárez, the town is something from which to gain satisfaction and so are the people in it. Wide sidewalks and small cars make it possible to have outdoor cafés and open areas where people congregate and enjoy each other's company. León spends a lot of time in the evening meeting his friends over coffee or a beer in their favorite café on the Plaza Allende. Since the Mexicans savor and participate in the town itself—its varied sights, sounds, and smells and its wide sidewalks and large park—the need for insulating space in cars is less than it is in the United States. Cars made in the U.S. are larger not just for economic reasons; they also separate the passengers and give them more personal room or more privacy. In the smaller Mexican cars, there is less space between the passengers, which gives them more opportunity to speak and to touch each other.

Mexican cities are organized physically and culturally in the model that Edward T. Hall calls a "radiating star."[1] That is, everything reaches out from the center—traffic, economic power, and influence. This system draws activities and functions to the center. On the other hand, the system of a grid, commonly found in the U.S., tends to string things out, separating functions and activities. In Altagracia, most power, influence, and control extend from the center of the town, specifically from the area of the square. Around the square are found the centers of government, of the police, of the courts, of the Church, and of the economy. The plaza is also a center for social activities and entertainment. Although today there is a bypass, the main highway still passes by the south side of the square.

As can be seen, A, B, and C are all pulled to the center as a meeting point in the radiating star pattern. However, in the grid pattern, there is no natural central point to attract them. Altagracia, like most Mexican towns, follows the radiating star pattern.

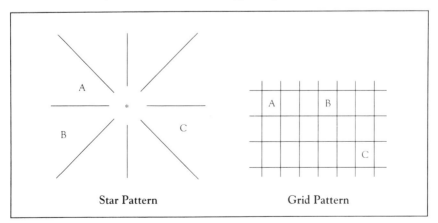

Star Pattern   Grid Pattern

1. *The Hidden Dimension* (Anchor Books), 1969. Although his research was based on French examples, the same characteristics are found in Mexico.

⌂⌂⌂ 2. ⌂⌂⌂

Housing

A. Old Houses

Many old colonial-style houses grace the center of Altagracia. The three generations of don Ramón López's family live in one of these once-elegant homes. These old homes were meant to shelter large, extended families. They are still very comfortable homes and are very well suited to the climate. Generally the houses extend right to the sidewalk in the front, where they display an imposing façade. In the front these old houses have a large wooden door, sometimes beautifully carved, called the street door (*la puerta de la calle*). A large metal knocker, usually made of bronze and often formed in a decorative shape, on the door greets the eye. Sometimes it is in the shape of an animal, such as a lion's head. To the sides of the front door are two or more windows. Often these windows come down to within two or three feet of the ground and reach upward eight to ten feet. Covering the windows are iron bars, or grillwork, with narrow spaces between them. On the inside of the house, the windows often have a ledge one can sit on to look out or where flowers can be placed. Also on the inside are two tall wooden shutters, which can be closed. Historically, these window ledges have also been "secret" meeting places for sweethearts. Eugenia Oteo, a high school student, often sits on the ledge to do her homework. Naturally, her younger brothers and sisters know she's really hoping that Jorge Luis will walk by and talk to her—and they tease her unmercifully about it. Eugenia met him at a church party, but, since they go to different schools, she doesn't have many chances to talk to him. "If he comes by today," she thinks, "maybe I'll give him my phone number."

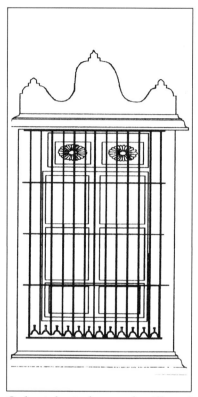

Colonial window and grillwork

Inside the front door of these old colonial houses, there is a small hallway (*zaguán*), closed by an inside door (*mampara*), which is a thin door that almost always is very delicate and beautiful. The top half usually has glass in it that is covered by a lightweight curtain. Inside the front door, facing the *zaguán*, are two large rooms whose windows face the street. One is usually a reception room for receiving visitors and the other is a music room. Beyond the inner door, there is a large central patio, which often has a fountain in its center. Scattered around the patio are trees, bushes, and many flowering plants.

The mild climate and abundant rainfall in Altagracia allow people to grow a large variety of plants and flowers in their open patios. Among the favorite plants, flowers, and bushes are bamboo, jade plants, large geraniums, gardenias, delicate ferns, petunias, spider plants, palm trees, different colored bougainvilleas, rubber trees, grape vines, poinsettias, and azaleas.

Along the sides of the patio, usually covered by a roof but open to the patio, are two long hallways that lead to other rooms, such as the

A colonial door knocker

dining room, the bedrooms, and a living room. At the rear are the kitchen and a pantry.

Today, some of these lovely old colonial homes have been converted into shops, serving as an attractive setting for the display of clothing, paintings, furniture, and decorative items. Also, some old homes now serve as boardinghouses or apartments.

Alicia Ruiz has converted one of these homes into a dress boutique that specializes in wedding dresses and gowns for special occasions. "It's an irony of life," says Alicia to her friends. "Here I am, selling wedding dresses, and I have yet to wear one myself!" An enterprising young woman, Alicia studied business and fashion at the university and she makes two or three trips a year to Europe and the United States to keep up on the latest fashions. Although business has been slow, Alicia has hired several clerks and accountants to help with the store and a maid and handyman to keep the lovely old house in mint

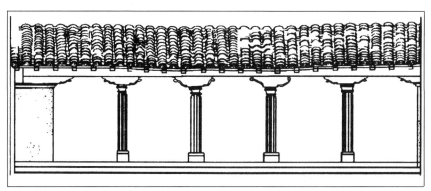

Patio hallway of a colonial house

Flowers in a patio

condition. "This house is the perfect romantic setting for lacy dresses and elegant gowns," she exclaimed when she first saw it.

B. Newer Houses

In the center of the town, there are a few modern buildings with apartments. None of them is taller than two stories. Although the buildings are modern, their façades conform to the old, colonial style.

The general scarcity of wood in Mexico, especially softwoods, and Hispanic traditions of housing have led to building methods and materials that are quite different from those in the United States. Modern houses or buildings are constructed with a framework of reinforced concrete pillars. Builders place these pillars about six to eight feet apart and set them on a platform of concrete which they previously poured on the ground, with foundations going down into the ground around the edges. Either reinforced concrete beams or steel beams span the wide open spaces in large rooms or in garages. Builders then use brick to fill in the spaces in the walls between the pillars, and they also use brick in the ceilings to fill in the spaces between the beams. Builders cover the ceiling bricks, which seem to defy gravity, with three or four inches of concrete and then a layer of tile to form the flat roof. While the bricks in the ceilings are usually left exposed, builders cover the brick walls with plaster on the inside and with a stucco finish on the outside. Before they plaster the inside of the walls, they hollow out a space in the bricks in which to place the electrical wiring and the plastic tubing for the plumbing. The only items of wood are the door frames and doors, and in many homes even the doors and frames are made of steel, as are the window frames. As a finishing touch, the builders always cover the floors with decorative floor tiles.

Life for upper middle-class families is very similar to that of middle-class people in the United States or Europe. Families in this class will have a small car; their children may attend private primary and secondary schools; and they work as professionals (doctors, dentists, architects), managers, or businesspeople. The Gregorio Cantú family is a good example. He is a lawyer (*abogado*) who has built up a thriving practice. In the Cantú home, the family has a color television set, a refrigerator/freezer, and a microwave oven. His children have been after him for some time to buy them a VCR so they can see the latest music videos. Gregorio insists that they improve their grades at school first. The Cantús are typical of this social group which makes up from 20 to 25 percent of the population in Altagracia.

The living room

The dining room of an upper-class home

For middle-class families, the modern apartments in the center of town and the individual houses in newer neighborhoods (*colonias*) in the suburbs all have a similar floor plan. Most houses have no front yard at all; they come right up to the sidewalk. A few, farther out from the center of town, have small front yards with a four-foot high wall and a gate at the sidewalk. The houses are attached to the neighboring houses on both sides. Since they have double walls, there is seldom a problem with noise from the neighbors. All windows are covered with wrought-iron bars for security, and the front door is a very heavy wooden door that is secured with a sliding bolt or bar, in addition to a lock.

The door to the street enters directly into the dining room (*el comedor*), which is furnished with heavy, colonial-style wooden table and chairs. Most rooms have either no curtains at all over the windows or only small decorative curtains to the sides of the window. To control the light, venetian blinds (*persianas*) are used. The floors are covered with attractive floor tiles instead of carpets.

Behind the dining room is the living room (*la sala*). Many Mexican

Furniture and tile floor

families keep the living room locked most of the time. It is used only for special occasions. The family is very proud of the sofa, the big chair, and above all, the console with the record player in it. To protect this furniture and to keep it new, they rarely use it. The López family recently used their living room for the fiftieth wedding anniversary of the grandparents, don Ramón and doña Elvira.

Behind the living room is the kitchen (*la cocina*). A hallway from the dining room leads to several bedrooms (*las alcobas*) and a bathroom (*el baño*), which has no bathtub, only a shower (*una regadera*) for bathing. Behind the kitchen or on the roof, there are quarters for the maid that virtually all middle-class families employ. The maid's quarters consist of a tiny bedroom and an even tinier bathroom. On the flat roof, hidden from public view by five-foot walls, are laundry facilities: a sink for washing and lines for drying clothes.

Due to the mild climate in Altagracia, central heating systems are not used. To provide some heat during the winter months, when the temperatures can occasionally drop down into the forties at night, families use small, portable propane or kerosene heaters. These heaters can be moved from room to room as needed. Some families have connected small heaters to the propane tanks in the patio in order to have a greater supply of fuel.

Today most middle-class houses have a small patio at the rear. Five-foot high metal cylinder tanks stand in one corner of the immaculate rear patio. These tanks, connected by metal piping to the kitchen and bathroom, supply the propane fuel needed for cooking in the kitchen and supplying hot water for both the kitchen and the bathroom. In some cases, the patio serves as an area for washing clothes. However, in other houses, the patio has been planned so that one or more bedrooms have a view of it. Sometimes these bedrooms will have sliding glass doors that open onto the patio. Most patios are small, perhaps 20 by 30 feet. The six-foot high walls that surround them make them very private. The patios are meticulously decorated with grassy areas, plants, flowers, and bushes. Many houses will have a cover over part of the patio to provide shade in the heat of day. This covered area is a favorite spot to place the birdcages that many Mexicans are so fond of. Canaries and parrots entertain the family with their song or their talk. At night the birdcage is covered and taken into the house.

The furniture in middle- and upper-class homes usually has a heavy framework of exposed hardwood. Sofas (*los sofás*) and large chairs (*los sillones*) have cushions that rest on a network of steel springs that is connected to the hardwood frame.

C. Housing for the Poor

The housing options for lower-class people are very limited in Altagracia. In town, they live in older homes that have been converted

Housing in poorer areas

into multiple residences, a few blocks from the city's center. Often an entire family of six to eight people will live in a single room and share a bathroom and kitchen with four or five other large families.

Some poor families have constructed "temporary housing" in vacant lots near the edges of the town or in one of several small shantytowns outside the city limits. These shanties have dirt floors, walls of adobe or cardboard and tin, a roof of tin held down by rocks, and only a single light bulb for light. For cooking and heating, the families use charcoal braziers (*braseros*). The bathroom is an outhouse with a hole in the ground. For drinking and cooking, families must carry water in buckets from a community faucet a block away. During the day, old men lead donkeys loaded with charcoal (*el carbón*) through the streets of these neighborhoods. The people use the charcoal for fuel.

Fuel coming in from the countryside

🏠🏠 3. 🏠🏠

Shops and Shopping

A. Clothing

Shoes are sold in a variety of locations. Around the main square, several shoe stores cater to the upper middle class, the tiny upper class, and visitors who have money. As the two names—"Zapatería Norma" and "Zapatería de Casa"—indicate, they are modern shops with attractive display windows (*vitrinas*) and well-dressed clerks. Norma Macías operates "Zapatería Norma," which has been in her family for two generations. Like many Mexican men and women, she believes that shoes reflect a person's character. Although her husband Oscar, a government worker, does not share her passion for shoes, he rarely lets a day pass without having his shoes shined or buffed by one of the bootblacks in the plaza. In Norma's shop and in the other shoe store, the emphasis is on fashion and elegance in men's and women's shoes. Of course, the prices are comparable to similar shops in larger cities, and there is no bargaining. Women's leather shoes are available in beautiful colors, such as jade or burgundy. While most of the shoes are made in Mexico, some are imported from Europe or Brazil. Because most Mexican women have small feet, it is difficult for American or European women to find shoes large enough for them in the Mexican stores.

Lower middle-class people and poor people look for shoes in stands that specialize in shoes in the municipal market. These are tiny stands, perhaps ten feet wide and ten to fifteen feet deep. The illumination for a stand comes from a light bulb hanging from a single electrical wire, and the shoes are displayed on cardboard boxes or on flimsy wooden racks. Additional display space is made by tying shoes

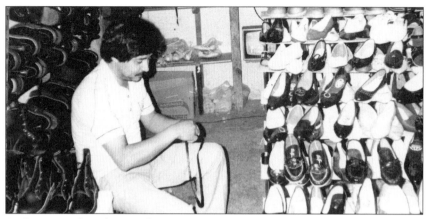

A shoe stand in the market

together by the laces and then hanging the pair from hooks that are attached to poles. Dozens of shoes can be displayed on poles standing upright inside the stand.

There is little variety in these stands, although some of them do feature a particular type of shoe, such as sandals (*huaraches*) worn by poor field workers, heavy work shoes worn by workers in plants and workshops, and simple, heavy-duty black oxfords that lower middle-class people wear. In the market, prices are not fixed, and customers must bargain (*regatear*) with the clerk to set a price that is agreeable to both. People also can find shoes at certain street markets and at curbside where traveling vendors park their pickup trucks and display their wares on boxes or on a folding table. Again, there are no set prices and the customers must bargain with the vendors.

Various kinds of shops sell clothing. As is true with shoes, attractive shops on or near the main square offer a variety of clothing for sale. Many of the women's fashions are one-of-a-kind items. They are handmade and very elegant. These ornate clothing items are colorful and sophisticated.

The shop "Ropa y Novedades Eloy" sells men's shirts, ties, socks, hats, pants and jackets. Across the square, the shop "Regalos El Edén" offers women's clothing such as blouses, skirts, dresses, silk scarves, shirts, swimsuits, and cosmetic items, including lipstick and eye shadow. The shop also carries creams, powders, and everything else that the fashion-conscious woman would want for her face and hair. The makeup runs from the basic to the dramatic. Middle-class Mexican women dress carefully before going shopping, and makeup is an important concern. A middle-class woman in Altagracia never goes shopping without being appropriately attired. It is just not acceptable to wear old clothes, to dress in shorts, or to appear in public without makeup or with hair in curlers.

The shop "Super Foto—Regalos" sells film and film services in addition to gift items, such as bags, men's clothing, and accessories, such as cufflinks and tie pins. The shop also sells some jewelry, crystalware, and porcelain items. As an added service, the clerks will giftwrap the purchases.

Many clothing items are made to measure in Mexico. Two fabric stores are located a block from the square. They carry enormous rolls of fabrics and large, commercial-style spools of thread wound around cones about eight inches high. They also display a large selection of yarn for knitting and floss for embroidery, as well as other handwork items.

When Teresa López wants a new dress, she goes to a fabric store and selects fabric and a dress pattern. Although many Mexican women sew their own clothes, Teresa never learned to sew, so she relies on a seamstress (una costurera) to make her skirts, blouses, dresses, and just about anything else she might need.

Teresa has been going to Aura Méndez for several years. Like many other seamstresses, Aura has set aside one room in her house where she meets customers, does the cutting and sewing, and holds fittings. Her sewing machine is a large, commercial machine used by professionals. Teresa has recommended her services to several friends, so Aura now has a thriving business.

Sometimes, customers come to her with only a picture of a dress or blouse they liked in a fashion magazine. Aura measures them, and with only the picture to guide her, she creates a pattern out of sheets

Conversion Table of Clothing Sizes									
Women's Clothes				Men's Clothes					
Dresses		Shoes		Jacket		Collar		Shoes	
Mex	US	Mex	US	Mex	US	Mex	US	Mex	US
36	6	3	5	48	38	36	14	$6^1/_2$	$8^1/_2$
38	8	$3^1/_2$	$5^1/_2$	50	40	37	$14^1/_2$	7	9
40	10	4	6	52	42	38	15	$7^1/_2$	$9^1/_2$
42	12	$4^1/_2$	$6^1/_2$	54	44	39	$15^1/_2$	8	10
44	14	5	7	56	46	40	16	$8^1/_2$	$10^1/_2$
46	16	$5^1/_2$	$7^1/_2$	58	48	41	$16^1/_2$	9	11
48	18	6	8	60	50	42	17	10	12

of newspaper. After fitting the pattern to the customer, she then creates the finished masterpiece—as lovely as anything customers would find in a boutique. Also, as Teresa has told her friends, the total cost is usually lower than the prices in stores and the clothes fit much better.

Whenever Rogelio López wants a suit or pants, he goes to a tailor (*un sastre*). The tailor carefully measures Rogelio and questions him about the style and fabric he wants. As Rogelio answers, the tailor jots down all the information and begins to work. Rogelio returns several times for fittings so that the suit will fit him perfectly and hang well. He has never been disappointed.

In contrast, poor people go the market to look for clothing such as work shirts and pants and one-piece cotton dresses. Also, street markets carry a wide variety of clothing items, especially on Sundays. There, these people can find clothes for the entire family. The clothing of the poor is always washable and very durable.

The clothing of poor people is very predictable. Poor men out in the countryside wear sandals, light cotton pants, and long-sleeved shirts, as well as a wide-brimmed hat. Poor men in Altagracia may wear sandals, but inexpensive leather shoes are more common, and tennis shoes are becoming increasingly popular. In town, they wear cotton or synthetic pants and shirts. They don't wear a hat, unless it is an American-style baseball cap. Sometimes they wear a light jacket (*una chamarra*). Poor women invariably wear a loose-fitting, one-piece dress, which may be made of cotton or a synthetic fabric. Over the dress they usually wear a large apron (*un delantal*), and around

A jewelry store

their shoulders a shawl (*un rebozo*). If the woman has a baby, it is wrapped in the *rebozo* and carried on her back. This leaves her hands free to continue working. Many women either wear sandals or they wear light canvas shoes.

B. Gifts

In addition to the gift shops already mentioned, there are two variety shops called *mecerías* that sell clothing, some fabrics, suitcases, shampoos, and creams. Shops that sell baby clothes and baby supplies are called *boneterías*. There is also a shop called "Abarrotes y Vinos" that sells foods and wines that could be used as gifts. Of course, under the arches at the north end of the square, there are stands that sell gift items such as inexpensive jewelry, toys, and candy. There is a jewelry store called "Platería Julio" that makes jewelry from silver. The store has many beautiful items, such as earrings (*aretes*), necklaces (*collares*), and rings (*anillos*). It also carries gold jewelry and other expensive gifts. Many items are fashioned to include semiprecious stones. From the outside, one would never guess that the store contained such glittering treasures.

C. Food

In the center of the town, several shops sell food items. These shops cater to the middle- and upper-class residents. The "Abarrotes y Vinos" store on the square has a selection of food items, candies, and

A mini supermarket

wines. A half block from the square, the "Tienda El Autoservicio" is a self-service store that provides a good selection of food and drink items, as well as newspapers and cleaning supplies. These two stores both provide shopping carts and have modern check-out areas. They have many packaged and canned foods, as well as condiments and delicacies. The prices there are much higher than in the market, and there is no bargaining. Rogelio and Teresa López shop there only for specialty items that can't be found in the market.

D. The Market

The town market, called simply *el mercado*, is located several blocks to the west of the square on San Pedro Street. Although the concept of a central market area goes back to pre-Hispanic times, this market is a fairly modern, concrete and brick building. This large market operates from around eight in the morning until about nine at night. However, since the individual stall or stand operators are independent contractors, they come and go as they please. Only about a third of them open at eight, and a few of them will still be open after nine at night.

The market is a place where all manner of merchandise is bought and sold. The main products are fruits, vegetables, meats, fish, chicken, and canned, bottled, and packaged foods. Also found are milk and cheese and clothing and household items. For those who might be hungry, there are food stands, fresh fruit juice stands, and stands selling snacks. For those looking for a gift, there are jewelry stands and handicraft items, such as *piñatas* (papier-mâché figures of birds and animals) and ceramics.

A fruit juice stand in the market

A fruit stand in the market

The market is organized into general areas. For example, the fruit stands are in one area, vegetable stands in another, fresh flowers in still another, and so on. The Álvarez family owns and operates one of the fruit stands. Everyone, except two-year-old Chemito, works or helps out at the stand. The father, Domingo, works at the stand whenever he is not needed at the local factory. Between the fruit stand and Domingo's job, the family manages fairly well.

The individual stands are small, about ten by ten feet. Facing the public, there is a counter or boxes containing samples of the merchandise. Around the sides, hanging above the stall, or sitting on shelves, are more display items. A single light bulb hangs overhead to provide light. The fruits and vegetables shine from being polished and are decoratively arranged to catch the eye. Samples of fruit are cut open to release an aroma that tempts the shopper's palate. The people who sell these products directly to the consumer are the same ones who raised them. Sacks with vegetables, colorful clothing items, clay containers, plants, wicker baskets, different kinds of meats and foods are all offered by vendors hawking their wares in loud voices.

There is activity every day, but on the weekends the market really comes to life. *El mercado* is a true spectacle, noisy and colorful. Most of the customers are from the lower class. These people don't go to the grocery stores in town. They come to the market, looking for fresh fruits and vegetables at cheap prices. The most important food items for the poor are corn tortillas, beans (*frijoles*), rice (*arroz*), and chili peppers (*ajíes*). They eat little meat, unless they live on a piece of land

Inside an appliance store

outside town and can raise some chickens or a pig. One interesting food is the cactus. The flat, broad leaves of the cactus are called *nopales*, while the smaller round buds are called *tunas*. Cooks prepare both of these by scraping off the spines with a knife and cutting them into pieces. They are added to foods, eaten cooked, or made into candies.

Nevertheless, the market is a meeting place for all the social classes. It is an amazing sight. The vendors loudly announce their products, all of them trying to get the attention of the buyers and point out the qualities of their products. All of this is done in a happy atmosphere in which the relationship between people becomes familiar and warm, filled with a desire to enjoy the moment. A well-known practice is bargaining for prices. The vendor always asks for much more than he expects to get. The buyer, well versed in this activity, offers half the amount. Then they continue to bargain until both are satisfied. In these exchanges of offers and counteroffers, there is often an element of humor and much evidence of witty language.

All during the day, people deliver things they have made or raised to the shopkeepers in the market. Small land owners ride on third-class buses with burlap bags containing corn or potatoes. It is not unusual to see farm people carrying chickens or pigs on the bus. In the streets around the market, people drive small groups of pigs in front of them as they make their way to the market.

The variety of people that one sees is as great as the variety of the merchandise. Men and boys wait near the exits, offering to carry packages or heavy objects that have been bought. These men, called *cargadores*, offer their services to people as they leave. Well-dressed women shop accompanied by their maids who carry bags in which the ladies place their purchases. Poor children run and play throughout the market. If the vendors are not alert, a child will snatch an apple and disappear into the crowd. The customers see signs of poverty near the exits—namely, men and women who, because of unemployment, advanced age, or handicaps, ask for a handout. Unofficial (not authorized) vendors approach people outside the market, offering them merchandise of doubtful quality. Other vendors offer herbs or strange substances that promise to improve your health, allow you to earn more money, or win back a lost love.

A visit to the market is an experience that leaves a deep impression on people from more developed countries who are not accustomed to being in direct contact with the sources and suppliers of their foods. This noisy, multicolored market is a representation of an entire society. The predominant impression that remains with a visitor to the market on a busy day is one of enjoyment in which the most important things are human beings and the relationships between them.

E. Specialty Stores

Altagracia also has specialty-type food stores. Included among them are a delicatessen (*salchichonería*), meat markets (*carnicerías*), bakeries (*panaderías*), tortilla stores (*tortillerías*) where fresh tortillas are sold daily for only two or three hours, ice-cream stores (*neverías*), candy stores (*dulcerías*), and a health food store (*una tienda naturalista*).

F. Street Markets

The government of Altagracia rents space to vendors in public areas so that vendors can set up tables, put canvases overhead for protection from the heavy summer rains, and run electric wires to nearby houses or stores where they connect to the electric power. Some of these street markets (*ferias*) are permanent, such as the long line of fruit and vegetable stands that operate in the street in front of the Loreto Church of San Pablo Street. These stands have some of the best-looking fruits and vegetables in town. At about nine P.M., the vendors close shop by placing heavy plastic sheeting over their merchandise and tying it down with numerous ropes in case a high wind

A street market stand

comes up. When you walk by these closed stands late at night, you can occasionally hear voices coming from inside. Edilberto Suárez and his sons often spend the night at their stand. Especially when there is some festivity in town, Edilberto prefers to protect his precious merchandise from rowdy revelers, as well as from robbers. By seven the next morning, Edilberto's sons are untying everything and getting ready to do business. When shoppers buy from these street vendors, they must be very careful and bargain well. The vendors have been known to overcharge or shortchange their customers.

Other street markets are temporary. Some of these are set up just one day a week, usually on public property. On Tuesdays, down Diezmo Street, is a "Tuesday Market" (*la feria del martes*). At this weekly market vendors sell fruits and vegetables, pots and pans, cosmetics, sewing machines, and blenders and other appliances. There is even a flea market of used tools and hardware, some of them good enough to be called antiques. They also sell used clothing, clothing seconds, and fried pigskin (*chicharrón*) to eat. Of course, many audiocassettes of popular music are for sale. However, many of them are illegal copies. In the week preceding Three King's Day (*el día de los Reyes Magos*) on January 6, San Pedro Street and the open market area are lined and covered with fast-erected canvas booths, selling toys, baby clothes, and nail polish. Throughout the week before All Saints' Day on October 31, there are similar booths selling sugar skeletons or miniature baskets of sugared fruit and flowers, a confectioner's delight. These temporary markets are amazing in their efficiency. Vendors arrive at the location about six in the morning, carrying all their wares in old trucks. In 30 to 40 minutes, they have stretched their canvases, which they tie to nearby houses, churches, or stores; they have set up their tables and stands; and they have laid out their merchandise for inspection. At about seven in the evening, they take everything down just as quickly. After they have loaded all their belongings on their trucks, they sweep the street and pick up all the trash. By eight o'clock, it is difficult to believe that just hours before there was a bustling scene of commercial and social activity.

An electrical hardware shop

♔♖♗♘ 4. ♗♖♗

Transportation

A. The Bus Station

The Bus Station (*Terminal de Autobuses*) is located on Allende Street three blocks south of the square. Since most people in Mexico travel by bus, even small towns like Altagracia have fairly large and modern bus stations.

There are different classes of buses that operate throughout Mexico. The first-class buses offer several advantages. Not only are these buses cleaner and more modern, they also have air-conditioning, a bathroom, and stereo music coming from speakers in the roof. In addition the seats are assigned, and riders may reserve their seats a day in advance. The companies also do not permit people to stand in the aisles. The cost for first-class service is not much more than that for the other classes, and riders are more likely to find a bus that is going straight through (*directo*) to the larger cities.

Generally, in second-class buses, seating is on a first-come, first-served basis. Also, people are allowed to stand in the aisle, which they will do even on ten- and twelve-hour trips. The buses are older and not as clean as the first-class buses; there is no bathroom; and people sometimes board with their bags of agricultural products, including chickens. Second-class buses do have several advantages, though. They serve smaller towns much more frequently than do the first-class buses, they are cheaper, and they often have separate bus stations in larger cities that are closer to the business section of town. The first-class station might be located in more of a residential section. Late at night, when the demand is not heavy, second-class buses provide a good choice.

There are also local rural buses that could be called third-class buses. They are sometimes referred to as "chicken buses" because of the many people who board them with chickens, rabbits, small pigs, or small goats. These buses all have a large luggage rack on the roof where animals and sacks of farm produce are carried. These buses are only for the adventuresome and hardy. Riders find themselves jammed into a bus meant to hold only half the number that manage to get on. And unsuspecting riders may find themselves sitting next to some chickens or even a pig.

Bus service is one of the strongest areas of private enterprise in Mexico. Although prices are fixed by the government, there is fierce competition in the areas of schedules and the quality of service. The names of the different bus companies are usually very colorful.

The following are sample schedules of bus service to Altagracia.

FIRST-CLASS SERVICE

A. Carrier "Tres Estrellas de Oro" (Three Gold Stars)

1. To Mexico City. Leaves Altagracia daily at 9:30 A.M. and arrives in Mexico City at 1:00 P.M. at the Terminal Norte station. (Mexico City has four huge bus stations, each serving a different area of the country.)

2. To Guanajuato. Leaves Altagracia at 1:30 P.M. and 6:30 P.M. daily. Arrives in Guanajuato at 3:00 P.M. and 8:00 P.M. This bus continues on to Tijuana through Guadalajara.

A second-class bus

A city bus

B. Carrier "Ómnibus de México"

1. To Guanajuato. Leaves Altragracia at 11:00 A.M. daily. Arrives in Guanajuato at 1:00 P.M.

2. To Mexico City. Leaves Altagracia at 12:00 P.M. Arrives in Mexico City at 3:30 P.M. at the Terminal Norte station.

3. To Guadalajara. Leaves Altagracia at 12:00 P.M. Arrives in Guadalajara at 6:30 P.M.

4. To Querétaro. Leaves Altagracia at 7:00 P.M. Arrives in Querétaro at 8:00 P.M.

If there is not a convenient departure by first-class bus from Altagracia, travelers often take the local second-class buses, which leave every 15 or 20 minutes, to Querétaro. Since the station in Querétaro is much larger and the city is located on the main highway between Mexico City and Guadalajara, there are frequent first-class departures to major cities.

SECOND-CLASS SERVICE

A. Carrier "Flecha Amarilla" (Yellow Arrow)

1. To Mexico City. Leaves Altagracia daily at 1:30 A.M., 2:00

"And all of this because of not studying"

A.M., 5:55 A.M., 7:00 A.M., 8:00 A.M., 9:40 A.M., 10:20 A.M.,
1:30 P.M., 2:30 P.M., 2:50 P.M., 3:50 P.M., 4:50 P.M., 5:40
P.M., 6:50 P.M., via San Juan del Río and Querétaro with arrivals in Mexico City about three and one-half hours after departure.

2.   To Querétaro. Leaves Altagracia every 20 minutes from 5:20
A.M. to 9:30 P.M. Arrival is about one hour after departure.

3.   To Aguascalientes. Leaves Altagracia daily at 10:30 A.M.,
2:30 P.M., and 5:00 P.M. Arrival is about three and one-half
hours after departure.

4.   To Guanajuato via San Miguel de Allende. Leaves Altagracia
daily at 6:30 A.M., 8:00 A.M., 12:00 P.M., 2:00 P.M., 3:00
P.M., and 5:00 P.M. Arrival is about two hours after departure.

5.   To Dolores Hidalgo via San Miguel de Allende. Leaves Altragracia daily at 5:00 A.M., 6:00 A.M., 8:00 A.M., 10:00 A.M.,
11:00 A.M., 12:05 P.M., 1:05 P.M., 2:05 P.M., 3:55 P.M., 6:00
P.M., 7:00 P.M., and 8:00 P.M. Arrival is two hours after departure.

6.   To León via Dolores Hidalgo and Guanajuato. Leaves Altagracia daily at 5:00 A.M., 6:00 A.M., 8:00 A.M., 11:40 A.M.,
12:05 P.M., 1:05 P.M., 2:05 P.M., 5:55 P.M., and 7:00 P.M. Arrival is about four hours after departure.

7.   To Morelia. Leaves daily at 8:00 A.M. and 11:00 A.M. Arrives
in Morelia about four hours later.

B. Carrier "Herradura de Plata" (Silver Horseshoe)

1. To Mexico City. Leaves Altagracia daily at 7:15 A.M., 8:00 A.M., 9:40 A.M., 10:20 A.M., 1:30 P.M., 2:30 P.M., 2:50 P.M., 3:50 P.M., 4:50 P.M., 5:40 P.M., and 6:50 P.M., via San Juan del Río and Querétaro with arrivals in Mexico City about three and one-half hours later.

2. To León via Dolores Hidalgo and Guanajuato. Leaves Altagracia daily at 5:15 A.M., 6:15 A.M., 8:15 A.M., 11:55 A.M., 12:20 P.M., 1:20 P.M., 2:20 P.M., 6:10 P.M., and 7:15 P.M. Arrival is about four hours after departure.

There are also more than a dozen smaller "chicken buses" that serve small country villages located within a forty-mile radius of Altagracia.

Because there are many buses coming and going from the bus station, the crowded conditions make it difficult for the drivers to back out of the loading ramps and leave the station. To guard against accidents, buses that back up are accompanied by a man or boy who walks behind the bus. This person carries a metal rod in his hands. With this rod he raps on the rear bumper of the bus, producing a noise that can heard for some distance. As long as the driver can hear the tapping noise of the metal rod, he continues backing up. If he no longer hears it, he stops at once. This system works very well, especially in the larger cities where the crowding is severe.

Once a year, Teresa López and her children Irene and Tomás travel to Guadalajara to visit Teresa's parents. Teresa isn't especially fond of bus travel, but her two children always enjoy riding the "Ómnibus de México." Because the bus leaves at noon, Teresa always packs a lunch for herself and the children. She is not sure which the children enjoy more, the six-hour bus trip or the visit with their grandparents.

The town of Altagracia operates a municipal bus system from six in the morning until ten at night. These city buses either have a sign above the windshield that indicates their routes or they have the route name painted on the windshield itself, opposite from the driver's side. A ride costs 350 pesos (about twelve cents). When riders pay the driver, he tears a numbered ticket off a roll. Riders keep their tickets because occasionally an inspector gets on the bus to make sure that everyone has paid the fare.

B. The Train Station

The Train Station (Estación de Ferrocarriles Nacionales) is south of town, about ten blocks from the square on Núñez Street. For many years, the railroads were not considered a good means of travel. The government had neglected the system for so long that the equipment and the roadbed were in very poor condition. In recent years, however, the government has purchased some secondhand Amtrak equipment, and service has improved greatly on some routes. The best service at the moment is the train called the "Blue Train" (*el Tren Azul*).

TRAIN SCHEDULE FROM ALTAGRACIA

A. Blue Train

1. To Mexico City. Leaves Altagracia at 5:00 P.M. daily. Arrives there at 9:00 P.M.

2. To Altagracia from Mexico City. Leaves Mexico City at 7:35 A.M. and arrives in Altagracia at 11:30 A.M.

B. Regular Train (older)

1. To Mexico City. Leaves Altagracia at 1:09 P.M. and arrives there at 5:30 P.M.

2. To Altagracia, continuing on to Nuevo Laredo. Leaves Mexico City at 2:45 P.M. and arrives in Altagracia at 7:15 P.M.

The service on the regular trains is somewhat inferior. The trains are generally late, but since riders can't be sure they will be late, they must be at the station at the scheduled time, and then they wait. These trains have no diner or sleeper cars. However, they do have a *Primera Especial* class, which is supposed to be better than *Primera Clase* (regular first class).

The only other northbound trains in the area leave from the small town of Pozo Blanco, close to Dolores Hidalgo and accessible from Altagracia by car. Riders can make a reservation and buy a ticket in Altagracia at the train station or at the travel agency, "Viajes Pinto," next door to the "Farmacia Gómez." Trains leaving from Pozo Blanco have a dining car, club car, and Pullman sleeper cars and leave at 11:30 P.M. daily. For those who can't get a ride from a friend or family member, taxis also make the trip between Altagracia and Pozo Blanco.

C. Air Travel

Few people from Altagracia ever travel by air because there is no local airport. However, for the few locals who do fly and the visitors wishing to leave Altagracia, there are some possibilities. Of course, Mexico City is only three and one-half hours away by bus. Then it is necessary to take a taxi from the bus station to the Mexico City airport. A more direct way also exists. The "Agencia de Viajes Alfredo López" on Diezmo Street makes reservations for travelers to go directly to the airport in Mexico City in VW buses, called *combis*. The buses pick up passengers at their residence. The agency also takes reservations for return trips to Altagracia from the Mexico City Airport. When don Ramón and doña Elvira López took a trip to the United States to visit her sister, they arranged for a *combi* to take them from their house to the airport in Mexico City. "It costs more to take a *combi*," said don Ramón, "but at my age, I can't make my way around the big city as easily as I used to."

Both San Luis Potosí and León have airports. Both of these cities offer air service to numerous locations in Mexico and at least one flight a day to the United States.

D. Car Travel

Virtually all of the cars traveling the roads of Mexico are made in Mexico, except for the cars of American or Canadian visitors. The Volkswagen Company manufactures a full line of cars, including the

A busy street

Cars for sale

Beetle. This little car today is manufactured in only a few countries, including Mexico. In fact, Mexico exports VW Beetles to Germany. Ford, Chrysler, General Motors, and Nissan (Datsun) all have manufacturing plants in Mexico.

All well-to-do people have cars (some of them are luxury cars), and nearly all middle-class people have a car, usually a small one. Don Ramón has a fifteen-year-old Ford that has served him well. However, he has kept it in good condition in the family-owned repair shop. His sons, Rogelio and David, have tried to talk him into getting a new car, like theirs. Rogelio has a VW Caribe (called a Jetta in the United States), and David has a Ford Tempo. Don Ramón calls them show-offs and sticks to his old car; however, he rarely turns down an offer for a lift (*un aventón*) in one of their newer model cars.

Small businesses have an old car or truck that they use to make deliveries or to pick up merchandise. There are also large numbers of taxis and trucks for hire. Some of the taxis are four-door pickup trucks. That combination permits the drivers to load more luggage or packages while still accommodating five or six passengers.

E. Service Stations

Only the government-owned oil company, Pemex, is permitted to operate service stations (*gasolineras*) in Mexico. Foreign oil companies, such as Texaco or Pennzoil, are allowed to sell cans of oil and other automotive products at stores. At the Pemex service stations, the prices and the selection of fuels are the same everywhere in the country. There are two choices of gasoline for cars: *extra*, which is unleaded (*sin plomo*), and *nova*, which is regular or leaded (*con plomo*). *Extra* gasoline sells for 755 pesos a liter. That means to fill up a typical car would cost 30,000 to 40,000 pesos. Although that sounds like a great deal of money, 30,000 pesos is roughly equivalent to eleven U.S. dollars. One U.S. gallon is equal to 3.78 liters, so one U.S. gallon of Mexican *extra* would cost the equivalent of $1.00 U.S.

Besides gasoline, most Pemex service stations also sell diesel fuel. On the major highways, there are large truck-stop service stations that sell only diesel fuel. In addition, some service stations perform other services, such as lubricating (*el engrase*) cars and trucks and changing the oil. All Pemex service stations also have restrooms (*el servicio*) which are usually clean. However, many of them don't have any toilet paper, so most people carry some in their cars, especially if they are traveling.

Beginning in 1990, all cars manufactured in Mexico have been made to operate on unleaded fuel in order to cut down on the air pollution in the cities. This represents a big change, and it will take many years before a majority of the cars on the road use only unleaded fuel. Even though the new regulation has been in effect, it is difficult to find unleaded fuel in many rural areas. Even in the large cities, service stations often run out of *extra* gasoline. In Altagracia, only the Pemex station located just out of town on the highway to Querétaro, at the junction of the bypass, can be counted on to always have *extra*.

Most car owners in Altagracia have their car serviced at privately owned shops. For lubrication and oil changes, they go to "Lubricantes" on East Madero Street. At shops such as this one, the car owner has a selection of brands (*marcas*) of oil (*aceite*), and the mechanics do very good work. To make sure that the oil has been com-

A transport truck

Conversion Tables for Car Care					
Tire Pressure Kilos to Pounds		Kilometers to Miles		Liters to Gallons	
Mex.	US	Mex.	US	Mex.	US
2.1	32	10	06.2	1	0.62
2.0	30	20	12.4	4	1.06
1.9	28	30	19.0	10	2.64
1.8	26	40	25.0	15	3.97
1.7	24	50	31.0	20	5.28
1.6	22	60	37.0	30	7.92
1.5	20	70	43.0	40	10.56
1.4	18	80	50.0	50	13.20
		90	56.0		
		100	62.0		
		110	68.0		

pletely drained from the car, they put the air hose to the oil filler pipe and blow air under pressure into the engine. This causes an additional cup of oil to drain out. A *servicio completo* gets the vehicle washed (*el lavado*) inside and out, including the engine compartment and under the vehicle, and includes lubrication and an oil change.

For repairs on cars, there are two authorized dealers in town (Chrysler and VW), but inexpensive and expert repairs are done at a number of other shops. Two good shops for general repairs are the "Mecánica López e Hijos" on West San Antonio Street (owned by don Ramón López), and "Automóviles Altagracia," located on South Diezmo Street. The shop "Auto Servicio Garita" specializes in trans-

A truck getting washed

missions, while the shop "Llantera San Pedro" specializes in tires (*llantas*) and wheels (*ruedas*). The "Llantera" is a good place to go if you have a flat tire (*una llanta ponchada*).

Car parts (*refacciones*) are in good supply for cars made in Mexico. Owners of foreign-made cars may have to wait for parts to be shipped in. However, Mexican mechanics are very good at repairing old parts or finding substitute parts.

F. Driving in Mexico

For highway driving, it is important to know the meaning of the common regulatory signs, such as the following:

Principales Señales de Tránsito	**Main Traffic Signs**
Conceda cambio de luces	Dim your lights
Carril izquierdo sólo para rebasar	Left lane for passing only
Camino sinuoso	Winding road
Modere su velocidad	Slow down
Tope	Speed bump
No rebase en raya continua	No passing on continuous line
Entroque	Side road

Road signs fall into three or four typical patterns. The eight-sided stop sign is unique. Then there are rectangular information signs. These have a black background with white lettering. The following are examples.

1 Stop sign   2 Hospital   3 Parking

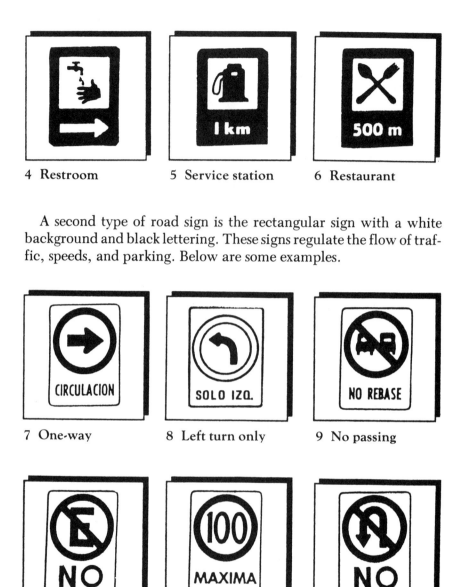

4 Restroom   5 Service station   6 Restaurant

A second type of road sign is the rectangular sign with a white background and black lettering. These signs regulate the flow of traffic, speeds, and parking. Below are some examples.

7 One-way   8 Left turn only   9 No passing

10 No parking   11 Speed limit   12 No U-turn

The third type of road sign is the warning sign. Warning signs are diamond-shaped, and most of them have no writing on them. They convey their message through effective drawings. Below are some examples:

13 Two-way traffic   14 Narrow bridge   15 School crossing

16 Workers ahead   17 Loose livestock   18 Slippery road

Teresa López has recently learned to drive and greatly enjoys her new-found mobility. She has mastered driving around Altagracia and finds that city driving holds no terrors for her, although she does not think she would attempt the traffic in Mexico City. She still feels a little insecure when she drives on the highways outside Altagracia, however, because the rules of the road and customs of driving are quite different on the highway than in town.

For example, on the highway, the use of turn signals is much different from in urban areas. In rural areas, especially with slow-moving trucks, the use of the left-turn signal by a truck in front of you is a signal that it is safe to pass. In fact, many turn signals on trucks have the word *siga* (go ahead, continue) on the left rear turn signal and the word *alto* (stop) on the right rear turn signal. That means that if the truck driver ahead of you is flashing his right turn signal, it is dangerous to pass.

It is dangerous to drive at night on the highways around Altagracia, especially the smaller ones that lead to out-of-the-way places. Usually, anywhere near a town, people and animals are walking along the highways at night. In fact, on desolate highways you might even find a donkey, horse, or cow sleeping on the pavement. Also, people who have old trucks or cars that break down often leave them sitting on the road for days with no sign or warning of any kind. People who repair their cars on the side of the road often put big rocks on the road to warn other drivers who might come along. Unfortunately, sometimes they drive away and leave the rocks in the road. The first time Teresa drove on the highway toward San Miguel, she didn't see some rocks left in the road until it was almost too late. She swerved in time to avoid damaging the car's underside, but the experience was enough to make her nervous about highway driving for some time.

When Rogelio Pérez's car broke down on the way back from Querétaro, he simply stayed with it and waited. The Mexican government has a system of roving trucks, called Green Angels (*Ángeles Verdes*), who come to the aid of stranded motorists. They usually help motorists with small repairs, sell them some gasoline, or give them a tow to the next town.

Violations of traffic laws are handled by the Transit Police (*Policía de Tránsito*). On the highway, highway patrol cars pull cars over when there is a violation (*una infracción*). However, in the cities and towns, most police officers are on foot. To get drivers to pull over, they blow their whistle and motion with their arm, indicating that you should pull over to the side of the road. If they are in front of you, they will step out in the street in front of your car to stop you. Once the driver is stopped, they ask to see a driver's license. If they decide to issue a traffic ticket (*una multa*), they keep your driver's license and turn it in at the police station. To get your license back, you have to show evidence you have paid the fine. Otherwise, they fear that few people would go in and pay their fines. For parking violations, they usually remove the car's license plates (*chapas de licencia*). Again you have to pay the fine to recover the plates. In Altagracia, the Transit Police share the police station (*la comisaría de policía*) on the Plaza Allende with the regular police.

An accident involving injury or property damage is a much more serious matter and is handled by the regular police. Until fault is determined in a contested case, both vehicles remain impounded. Often both drivers are held until they can appear before a judge. If the accident occurs at night, the drivers may have to wait in jail overnight in order to see the judge.

The highways in Mexico are being improved dramatically, although they weren't bad to begin with. Around 1985, Mexico launched an ambitious program of divided highway construction. This costly program is being financed by charging a toll (*una cuota*).

Placing the cost on the user was the only way that Mexico could embark on such a program during a time of high inflation and government deficits. The tolls seem high by U.S. standards. To drive one hundred miles may cost the equivalent of $1.00 in American money at the toll booth (*la caseta de cobro*). These divided highways bypass the cities and have limited access.

Today a motorist can drive from the U.S.–Mexico border at Nogales nearly all the way to Mazatlán on a divided highway. The remaining sections will soon be in service. From Mazatlán to Guadalajara, an enormous construction project is putting in a divided highway through the mountainous terrain that separates those two cities.

Receipt for a toll road

Â888Â 5. 8Â8

Public Services

A. The Post Office

The Post Office (*Oficina de Correos*) is located on the corner of Allende and Mesones streets, one block north of the square. The Post Office is open Monday through Friday from eight to six, and on Saturdays from nine to eleven. It is closed on Sundays and holidays. The Post Office sells stamps (*estampillas*) and postcards (*tarjetas postales*). Letters may be sent by land (*tierra*) or by air (*vía aérea*). At the counter (*mostrador*) to the left, packages (*paquetes*) may be sent. Both packages and letters can also be sent by certified mail (*certificado*). Mexicans consider it very bad manners to lick stamps with your tongue before putting them on your letter. One reason for this, of course, is that stamps are handled quite a bit by postal workers. To accommodate the mail patrons, the Post Office usually provides a small dish with a moistened sponge in it. To moisten a stamp, the customer merely rubs the back of the stamp against the moist sponge. Another device is a dish with water in the bottom and with a ceramic wheel that turns. The customer turns the wheel, causing it to be moistened, and then slides the stamp along the wheel.

The cost of stamps is about 88 cents in U.S. money for air mail to the United States and about 35 cents U.S. for local mail. The mail carrier either walks or rides a bicycle. Out in the rural areas, the carrier blows a whistle so the people know he is there. The sound of that whistle is unmistakable.

Another service provided by the Post Office is the rental of post office boxes (*apartados postales*). Since boxes are usually all rented out, customers must put their name on a waiting list. The renewal time is

January, which is the best time to inquire about a box.

Eugenio Barco has worked at the Post Office in Altagracia for five years. He often says that the best part of his job is being able to help people. A considerable number of people in Altagracia have relatives who live and work in the United States. Usually the relatives try to help out by sending money orders to family members in Mexico. Since Eugenio knows most of these family members, he lets them know as soon as the money order has arrived from the U.S. He also knows that for many of them, the money orders are their only source of income. It makes him feel good to know that he can help them in a small way.

B. Telephones

The Telephone Office (*Central Telefónica*) is located on Allende Street, just one-half block south of the square. The office is open from Monday through Saturday, from 8:00 A.M. to 1:30 P.M. All telephone numbers in Altagracia are formed by a single number, 2, followed by a dash and two numbers, followed by another dash and two more numbers—for example, 2–00–59. When twelve-year-old Tomás López calls his friend, Mateo Laguna, he dials 2–35–74. Tomás likes to use the phone so much that his parents have started placing time limits on his calls.

A long-distance station

A public phone

The office and the telephone exchange (*teléfono L.D.*) are two different entities. The first is where you go to arrange for the installation of a phone or for phone repairs. A customer must wait a long time for repairs to be made on a telephone, since there seems to be a shortage of workers. Because of a lack of available telephone numbers at the exchange, it may take several years to get a new line installed. Occasionally, someone who is moving away will agree to sell his or her phone to the person who is moving in. In that case, however, the new resident can't change the directory to show his or her name, since that would require going through the process of getting a new phone installed.

Since Mexico has gone through a period of extremely high inflation, all prices, including the cost of phone calls, rise regularly. To avoid the problem of having to change all public phones frequently to accommodate new prices, a system of tokens (*fichas*) is used. In this way, the price of the token can change without any change in the phone equipment. To make a call, the customer must first buy a token at a store. Then the customer inserts the token in the phone and makes the call.

The Telephone Exchange, next door, is where customers go to make long-distance calls, since they can't be made from regular phones. The hours of operation are from 10:00 A.M. until 10:00 P.M. Long-distance calls can be paid for in cash, they can be collect calls (*por cobrado*), or they can be paid for by a credit card. It is an interesting experience to make a long-distance phone call. At the exchange office, there are four phone booths around the room and a desk staffed by a clerk. The customer who wishes to make a call goes to the clerk and gives him or her the number he wants to call. The customer also indicates whether the call should be person-to-person or station-to-station. The clerk takes down the information and then tells the customer how long the wait will be, usually about twenty to thirty minutes. However, on holidays the wait can be several hours. There are ten or twelve chairs in the room where people sit while they wait. Sometimes whole families are present if a call is going to be placed to grandmother or some other special relative. When it is the customer's turn, the clerk tells the customer which booth (*cabina*) to go to and dials (*marca*) the number. After the call is finished, the customer returns to the desk. The clerk calls the company and finds out how many minutes were used, and then calculates the charges. The customer pays and the transaction is completed.

C. The Bank

All banks in Mexico were nationalized by the government in 1982, although they still conserve their old names. "Banamex" is located on the south end of the square on Insurgentes Street, "Banco Serafín" is on the west side of the square on Aldama Street, and "Bancomer" is also located on Aldama, one-half block north of the square. Although all are nationalized, some banks offer better rates or services than others. That means it's good to shop around.

Besides savings and checking accounts, banks also offer such services as changing money (from dollars to pesos, for example), holding trust papers, and collecting for utility bills. Since it is still not customary in Mexico to pay bills by sending checks in the mail, people can pay their utility bills at the bank. Most lower-class and lower middle-class people don't have bank accounts of any kind.

The hours of bank service are fairly limited. Banks are open from 9:00 A.M. until 1:30 P.M. Some services are even more limited than that. For example, money can be changed only from nine to eleven in the morning. Because many poor people have relatives who are living and working in the United States, it is not unusual to see a very poor-looking person pull out a one hundred dollar bill and exchange it for Mexican pesos.

In general, a lot of paperwork is involved in completing simple transactions in a Mexican bank. For example, to cash a traveler's check, it is necessary first to wait in line to see one of the supervisors of the bank who has a desk some distance from the tellers' windows. He or she examines all the identification carefully, verifies the signature, and then signs an authorization paper. The supervisor then hands all the paperwork to an employee who takes it to a teller's window. The client must stand in line at the teller's window until it is his or her turn to receive the money.

Alfredo Pinto, who owns the travel agency "Viajes Pinto," has learned to be a patient customer. He comes to the bank every day to deposit the previous day's receipts. Because of the bank's limited hours, he is forced to keep the money in an office safe overnight. Alfredo has tried to talk to the bank president about making special allowances for the local businesses. So far, though, he has not had much luck.

Besides the banks, there is one other business that changes money. It is the "Casa de Cambio" on Juárez Street between Insurgentes and Hidalgo. It is open from 10:00 A.M. to 10:00 P.M. Some hotels and businesses will also change money, but they don't offer rates as favorable as those of the banks or the money exchange.

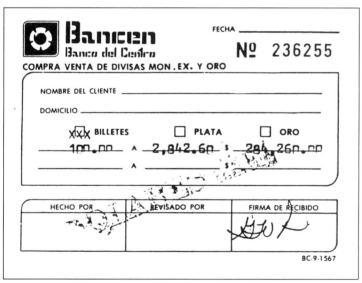

Receipt for changing money

⌂⌂⌂ 6. ⌂⌂⌂

Entertainment

A. The Movies

There is only one movie theater in Altagracia, the "Cine Madero," located on Allende Street, one-half block north of the square. A large marquee displays the names of the films, and windows to the sides of the ticket window (*la taquilla*) display posters of coming attractions. Most of the films are about cowboys or criminals.

Some wealthy people have satellite dishes on the roofs of their houses, allowing them to receive programs and movies from Europe or the United States. One hotel, the "Hotel del Virrey," shows English-language films one night a week. Once a month the high school English class goes to the hotel to watch these movies. The teacher, Graciela Hernández, says that the movies are an enjoyable way for the students to sharpen their listening skills.

B. The Park

Altagracia has a lovely park, called *el Parque Juárez*, located at the east end of Hidalgo Street. Only a few blocks from the center of town, the park has an abundance of vegetation—plants, flowers, and trees. Several paths crisscross the park, and city streets go completely around the park. This allows people to drive around and find a secluded spot for a picnic or a nap. Within the park, there are picnic tables, open areas for play, and children's playground equipment. The atmosphere at the park is one of unspoiled naturalness.

During the morning hours, men and women jog on these attractive paths; in the afternoons, mothers and maids go there on walks with children. To the west side of the park, there are several tennis courts (*canchas de tenis*) and a basketball court (*la cancha de básquetbol*). All day long people desiring physical exercise use these facilities.

Although the park has a fence around it with large iron gates at the main entrance, the gates are never locked.

C. The Café

There are several popular cafés in Altagracia that serve as social centers as much as they do as places to eat. At the "Parroquiano" on Insurgentes Street, Tomás López and his friends stop in for a soft drink (*refresco*) to enjoy along with a snack (*antojito*) on their way home from school. Carbonated soft drinks are available in apple, strawberry, grape, Coca-Cola, Pepsi, and orange. Other choices in beverages include several brands of mineral water and hot chocolate. The hot chocolate is usually served with whipped cream on top. Coffee can be black (*café solo*) or with cream (*con crema*). A favorite snack is a sandwich (*el sándwich*) with cheese and jam. Ladies out shopping might also stop in for a snack, such as a cup of tea and some cookies.

At "El Pegaso" on Hidalgo Street, working-class men stop in for a glass of wine, a bottle of beer, or a cup of coffee and chat (*charlar*) with friends. This café caters to men. It is plain and simple, with bare wooden floors and plain wooden tables and chairs. Women are not forbidden to enter, but they usually do not feel comfortable there. The language used there is the kind men use when they are alone. At one table, several men play a game of dominoes; at another, four men play a card game. At other tables, the men are talking or reading the newspapers they bought at a nearby news stand.

D. The Bullring

There is a bullring located south on Núñez Street. Because Altagracia is a small town, they do not have a formal bullfighting season. You must look for the announcements of bullfights (*las corridas de toros*) posted around town to find out the dates of the fights. All fights start at 4:00 p.m. and cost from $2.00 to $5.00 U.S. The more expensive seats are in the shade (*la sombra*). A bullfight is a great spectacle of pageantry and color. The most important bullfight of the year takes place the last week of September, at the time of the celebration of

Michaelmas. "El Matador" restaurant always displays many photos and posters of famous matadors and is a favorite eating place for the local fans.

Less formal events, called *novilladas*, are put on by aspiring fighters, who are usually in their mid to late teens. A *novillo* is a young bull. The animal is not killed in these events, since the purpose is to allow both the young bulls and the young bullfighters to show off their ability. In the bullfighter, the fans look for skill and courage; while in the bull, courage and determination are sought-after qualities. The admission price is much less for these events than it is for *la corrida*.

The Mexicans do not consider the bullfight as a fight between the person and the animal. The English term *bullfight* is really not a translation of the Spanish term *corrida de toros*, which means a "running of the bulls." The English term is a misunderstanding of the way Mexicans view the event. To the Mexicans it is a performance. They don't go to the bullfight to see who will win. Rather, they go to see the performances of the bull and the bullfighter. The *torero* who demonstrates courage, skill, and grace in the face of mortal danger will receive great applause. The bull that shows courage, stamina, and strength will also receive the admiration of the fans.

E. The *Charro* Ring

A *charreada* is similar to what is called a rodeo in the United States. In fact, it probably is the origin of the rodeo. The *charros*, or Mexican

A sidewalk news stand

cowboys, demonstrate their skills with the lariat (*la reata*) and with handling cattle. They also do "bulldogging," in which they dive from a horse, grab a steer by the horns, and then throw the animal to the ground. Another contest is tail twisting. In this competition, the cowboy on horseback, galloping at top speed, grasps the tail of a running steer and throws it to the ground. There are always *mariachi* singers who perform at the *charreadas*, which are held once a month.

A visit to a *charro* ring is a good place to see the sources of much of the equipment and many of the terms used in the horse and cattle industry in the Southwestern United States. The western saddle (*la silla*), the cinch (*la cincha*), the lariat (*la resata*), the lasso (*el lazo*), the horsehair rope (*el mecate*), and the quirt, or whip (*el látigo*) all derived from the Mexican influence in the Southwest before Mexico lost that territory to the United States in 1848. In the cowboy, the large hat (*el sombrero*), the boots (*las botas*), and the chaps (*los chaparejos*) have the same origin. The colors of horses, such as roan (*el roano*), bay (*el bayo*), and the pinto (*el pinto*) also come from Spanish. Other terms derived from Spanish are mustang (*el mesteño*), stray (*estraviado*), and stampede (*estampido*).

F. The Art School

The Art School is called "Bellas Artes" (Fine Arts). The building is a former monastery. Beginning with the revolutionary constitution of 1857 and reaffirmed in the constitution of 1910, all religious orders were prohibited, as were all religious vows. Throughout Mexico, former convents and monasteries have become museums, centers of tourist information, or schools of some kind.

The Art School in Altagracia is a beautiful two-story building, built around a large central patio. Certainly, the beautiful colonial buildings, the rural setting with deep blue skies, and the green countryside were a strong influence in attracting some painters. The Art School was founded about thirty years ago, and today there are art classes all day long. There are classes for children, for beginners, and for senior citizens. There are always foreign art students, mostly from the United States and Canada. The majority of the foreign art students come during the winter months to escape the cold northern weather.

In addition to painting, there is considerable activity in other arts, such as pottery making, jewelry making, singing, guitar playing, and

One patio at the art school

dancing. The dancing includes a lively folk dancing class and ballet. The Art School sponsors a folk dancing group that performs around the area.

Two or three times a month there are painting or photograph exhibits, dance or musical presentations, or special lectures. The building is open from 9:00 A.M. until 9:00 or 10:00 P.M. Visitors are welcomed, and many come in the afternoons and evenings to walk through the long corridors that open to the patio, stopping to look in all the different large rooms to watch the painters, musicians, or singers. It is worth a visit just to see the impressive building.

G. The *Teatro Nervo*

The Teatro Nervo, on Diezmo Street, is an older building that has been well maintained. It has seating for about 300 people. There are events of one kind or another held about once or twice a month. Usually the events are not theatrical productions, but musical programs, dance programs, or lectures. Last Wednesday, for example, there was a musical program presented by students from the "Instituto LaValle," a large private school in Mexico City. That school has educational programs from elementary through high school, and the students from all levels presented musical numbers. All the students came in three buses, and they stayed with local families who were arranged for by a cooperating school.

The entire López family—don Ramón and doña Elvira, their son David, and their son Rogelio with his wife Teresa and their children—all attended. Teresa and Rogelio had volunteered to house four of the visiting students, and they watched them as proudly as they would have watched their own children. Although some of the numbers by the smaller children were not very professional, everyone thoroughly enjoyed the program and gave the performers a warm round of applause. The program was long, more than two hours, but no one was eager to leave. The audience enjoyed one another as much as they did the program.

▲▲▲ 7. ▲▲▲

The Hospital and Health Care

A. The Hospital

The town hospital, *el Centro Médico de Altagracia*, is located on Núñez Street, between Insurgentes and San Antonio. While it offers a full range of services, including surgery, some people consider it as a place to go only for emergencies or minor problems. For serious medical problems, middle-class and upper-class people prefer to go to nearby larger cities. The closest large city is Querétaro, where the latest in medical technology is available. Other, larger cities with excellent medical facilities are Celaya and San Luis Potosí.

The Social Security system (*Instituto Nacional de Seguros Sociales*) does not cover all the people. Anyone who works at a factory, shop, or store that deducts the necessary payments and makes the matching contributions can belong. Since the daily minimum wage in Mexico is only about the equivalent of $3.50 U.S., the premiums are not very high. The Social Security system has its own system of hospitals throughout the country. However, in small towns like Altagracia, there isn't one. In Altagracia, people who are covered by Social Security are treated at the regular hospital at a greatly reduced rate. The Social Security (INSS) also pays for all the medicine and drugs for its members. Some people who belong to Social Security prefer to travel to Celaya or Querétaro to have hospital care or to see a specialist.

However, since many people are self-employed, such as gardeners, carpenters, and electricians, they often feel they cannot afford to make the Social Security payments and so they do not belong. In addition, many people either work at small shops or stores that won't participate or they don't work at all. This means that there are many people who have no health insurance at all.

The federal government also has a health-care system for all federal workers throughout the country. In the larger cities the government has its own hospitals and medical staffs. Since there is no federal hospital in Altagracia, the few federal workers who live here have an arrangement with the local hospital.

B. Private Clinics

There are several private clinics that are owned and operated by doctors. Two brothers who are doctors, Francisco and José Hernández, operate the "Clínica Santa María" on San Antonio Street. In addition to equipment for treating a variety of ailments, they also have some diagnostic equipment, such as X-ray and electrocardiograph machines. Next door to them is a medical laboratory, the "Laboratorio Altagracia," where technicians do blood and urine analyses as well as tests for pregnancies.

A doctor's office

There is also a maternity clinic on Madero Street. This is where middle-class women often go to have a baby. This private clinic is more expensive than the hospital, but the care is very good. Many other middle-class women go to the hospital for child delivery.

Most poor people have babies at home, attended by a midwife (*partera*). They can't afford the hospital, and home delivery is the only method they have ever known.

C. Ambulances

The Red Cross on San Pedro Street provides ambulance service and runs a small clinic. People who are injured on the highways or at work are usually brought to this clinic first. If the patients have insurance or can afford it, they are moved to the hospital. If they don't have insurance, they stay here, unless their injury is very serious.

If the Red Cross ambulances are all busy, the dispatchers will call the Fire Department ambulance. Because the town is fairly small, an ambulance usually arrives within ten minutes from the time of the phone call.

D. Doctors

There are some very good doctors in Altagracia. Compared to doctors' fees in the United States or Europe, their fees are very low. A visit to a doctor or a dentist can cost the equivalent of five to ten dollars. It is a good idea to ask friends and neighbors for recommendations. Dr. Manuel Bravo is a good example of a typical doctor. He has a general practice and sees patients at his office (*el consultorio*) on Aldama Street from 9:00 a.m. to 2:00 p.m. After the midday meal, he either makes house calls or visits patients in the hospital. If the patient needs medicine, he writes a prescription (*la receta*) to be filled at the pharmacy.

E. The Drugstore

There are four or five pharmacies (*las farmacias*) in Altagracia. Unlike drugstores in the United States, they sell only drugs, medicines, and a wide range of cosmetic items. Because most poor people seldom go to a regular medical doctor, pharmacies are allowed to sell all

La farmacia

drugs and medicines, except narcotics, without a prescription. It is not unusual to see a veteran pharmacist looking at the throat of a customer or examining the rash on a patient's leg. He will then recommend a medicine for them. The pharmacies take turns staying open late or on Sundays and holidays. The one that stays open is called *la farmacia de turno*.

F. Folk Medicine

Among many uneducated people, and even among a good number of people with some education, there are some widely held folk views about the causes and treatments of sickness. Because many of the poor people have had little or no formal education, they have never been taught that germs cause diseases. Instead, they attribute illness to other factors, such as bad luck, curses from God and others, imbalances in the body, and enchantments. They believe that good health is dependent on a balance between two sets of polar elements. The one axis is a contrast between hot and cold elements, while the other is a contrast between weak and strong elements.

When people get sick, it is because their bodies have been overloaded with one of the elements, and to restore health, they need elements from the opposite end of the line. Foods, beverages, herbs, medicine, animals, and even people are characterized by a quality of heat and cold. These characterizations do not always relate to either the temperature of the food or beverage or the hot spices they might contain. Sometimes actual temperatures are involved, as in overheating by the sun or chilling by water. Often, however, hot and cold are considered innate traits of a substance. For example, wheat, coconut, meat, ice, and the castor bean are hot items. Pears, milk, eggs, corn, potatoes, and watermelons are cold.

The condition called *calor subido* (risen heat) occurs when a person steps barefoot on a cold tile or cement floor or gets his feet wet in a rainstorm. The cold touching the feet pushes the heat upward from the feet, compressing the heat in the already warm upper parts of the body and producing excessive heat. This excessive heat in the head and upper torso manifests itself as any of a number of illnesses.

Strong emotions, such as anger, fear, envy, or joy can also bring on a dominance of heat. Certain activities or states allow the heat to rise to higher levels. Some of these are sleeping, eating, working with the hands or with the eyes (reading or needlework), pregnancy, and childbirth.

When a poor person becomes sick, he or she makes a self-diagnosis and takes a home remedy, such as teas or herbs. If the illness continues, the sick person consults a *curandero* (folk healer). As a last resort, he or she may go to a medical doctor. Poor people are reluctant to go to modern medical doctors. One reason is that it is very expensive for them, and another is that they feel completely out of place in their old, dirty clothes in the spotless medical clinics or hospitals where everyone is dressed in white. The doctors and nurses seem cold, distant, and even unfriendly. The medical professionals are middle- and upper-class people. They speak a more proper Spanish and they use strange-sounding medical terms. They sometimes make fun of the poor people's folk interpretations of the illnesses, they don't seem to want to touch them, and they try to hurry them out as quickly as they can. On the other hand, the *curandero* is usually someone the people know who treats them with kindness and tenderness. There is touching, often a massage, and nearness. The *curandero* is dressed as they are, he talks as they do, and he understands illness in the same way they do.

ᾆᾆᾆ 8. ᾆᾆᾆ

Sports and Recreation

A. Soccer

As in all of Latin America, soccer (*el fútbol*) is the most popular sport. Little children begin playing with a soccer ball when they are three or four years old. Poor children sometimes make a ball by tying old rags together in a ball shape. Small children spend many hours kicking a soccer ball in the streets in front of their houses, or in the patio inside their houses. Older children organize neighborhood games of soccer. By the time young boys are ten or twelve years old, they have developed a high level of skill with their feet. A demonstration of this is seen when two or three boys stand facing each other about four or five feet apart and try to keep a soccer ball in the air between them using only their feet. It is remarkable how long they can do this.

Many young men belong to neighborhood (*colonia*) teams. A group of fathers will get together and organize a neighborhood team. The organizers will obtain copies of the birth records of the players, along with a photo of each boy. Then they take these records to the city office where sports are organized. Most cities and even small towns sponsor three leagues. The first league (*liga*) for young children is the "Juniors" league. The second league for teenagers is called the *jóvenes* league. The third is for adults (*adultos*).

David López, who is a great soccer fan and a former player, organized a soccer team in the neighborhood where he and most of his relatives live. His nephew Tomás is on the team. David is also the coach for the team, *Las Águilas del Norte* (the Northern Eagles). The team members can always expect a good turnout from the López family to cheer them on.

67

Every vacant lot or field is used for soccer in the afternoons or on weekends. The fathers and boys improvise boundary lines and goalposts with sticks, rocks, and pieces of paper. Some of the fields have had considerable work put into them. They have permanent goalposts and painted rocks for boundary markers. The boys all have soccer shoes and a uniform, and they play with a regulation ball.

On weekends, neighborhood teams often board the intercity buses to travel to nearby towns to play soccer games. They all have a bag that contains their uniform and their soccer shoes. One time, David's team was a little short of money for the full bus fare for all the boys. David held a spirited conversation with the driver as he tried to work out a deal. Since the driver was a soccer fan himself, he accepted what money they had and forgot the rest.

Traveling on regional highways, one can see numerous soccer games taking place within view of the highway. Every town has a regulation soccer field with seating for four or five thousand fans. In Altagracia, the soccer field (*cancha de fútbol*) is located at the extreme west end of San Antonio Street. Banners in town announce that the town's all-star team will be playing an all-star team from Dolores Hidalgo on Sunday. There is much interest and it is certain that there will be a good turnout. A festive atmosphere surrounds these rivalries between towns. Vendors hawk popcorn, candy, peanuts, and cotton candy to the spectators. Other vendors sell children's toys, such as pinwheels (*estrellas*), plastic snakes, whistles, and animals. Soft drinks (*refrescos*) and beer (*cerveza*) are also popular items.

Among the men and boys in the town, there is enormous interest in the national and international soccer competition. When the World Cup Tournament is held, everyone who has a television set watches the games. All Mexicans were very proud when the World Cup games were held in Mexico in 1986.

Everyone knows the names of the international superstars. Many people read sports magazines and newspapers that give them information about the most prominent stars. All of the soccer fans (*aficionados*) impatiently await the arrival of Monday's newspaper which gives the results and stories about Sunday's games. Television and radio programs give sports updates and broadcast games live (*en vivo*). During one of these games, the streets appear deserted. When one of the teams scores a goal in the game, cheers can be heard coming from all the houses along the street. In cafés and clubs, groups gather to watch the games. In restaurants, stores, and shops, there usually is a television set showing the games. People try to watch the game out of the corner of their eye while they are working.

B. Basketball

After soccer, there is a big drop in popularity to the next sport. A long way down, the second most popular sport is basketball (*el básquetbol*). There are outdoor basketball courts (*canchas de básquetbol*) at the Parque Juárez and at the Education Complex at the south end of Juárez Street. A few middle-class homes have basketball hoops mounted on a pole in the driveway or in the patio. In the afternoons and on weekends, the basketball courts are very busy with impromptu games. There are also neighborhood teams that organize games. Although a large number of people play basketball, it still does not get much attention in the newspapers, radio, or television. One reason for the lack of publicity is that the schools don't sponsor teams. Likewise, there is no large court where large numbers of spectators can watch. Only during the Olympic Games or the Pan American Games do the television networks in Mexico broadcast basketball games. As a result, there are no national or international basketball stars in Mexico.

C. Baseball

Baseball (*el béisbol*) is more popular than basketball in the north of Mexico, and almost as popular as basketball in the *bajío* region. There are no regulation baseball fields in Altagracia. Like soccer, it is played mostly in vacant fields in town or on the edge of town. The children who play make their own field, clearing away rocks and brush, and leveling it as best they can. They use pieces of cloth or paper for the bases. Some of the boys have regulation leather mitts, while others have cut a piece of cardboard in the shape of a mitt and tie it on their hand with a string. Sometimes they use a wooden handle or other piece of wood for the bat. Regardless of the makeshift equipment, they play with tremendous enthusiasm. There are several neighborhood teams in town that play each other or that travel to nearby towns on weekends to play.

When David López was a youngster, he loved to play baseball. For five years, he and a group of friends played for the same neighborhood team, *las Medias Rojas* (the Red Socks). For two years in a row, they played for the town championship in the *jóvenes* division. No matter how hard or well they played, they never won the championship game.

D. Tennis

There are tennis courts in Altagracia in the Parque Juárez and at the Education Complex at the south end of town. The courts at these locations are occupied most of the time, except in the winter when the weather is too cold for outdoor sports. The "Hotel del Virrey" also has a tennis court and it sponsors a tennis tournament every year in June. Some players come to the hotel every year because of their love of tennis.

E. Running

Today, just as in the United States and Europe, Mexicans are concerned about good health and the need to exercise. There is an exercise gym on Aldama Street, "Thomas's International Gym," attempting to present a modern image with an English name. Even though it's in an old colonial building, it has a full set of weights and other exercise equipment. The gym advertises better physical appearance, better muscle tone, better health, and freedom from tension. Instructors also give advice on proper nutrition and on healthy foods. The gym has hours for men, women, and mixed groups.

The gym owner, Tomás Ibarra, lived in the United States for several years. He worked out in gyms there and decided that it would be a good idea to start one in Altagracia. So far, it has been very successful, but Tomás cannot quite understand why more women than men come to the gym to exercise.

People run (*correr*) or jog (*trotar*) in the Parque Juárez and on outlying streets. The most popular hours for running are early in the morning or late in the evening. Large numbers of people are not involved in this sport, but those that are wear sweatsuits (*las sudaderas*) and modern running shoes.

F. Swimming

The same "Hotel del Virrey" also has a swimming pool (*una alberca*) behind the hotel. At times when the hotel is not very busy, the man-

agers let people from town swim there for a fee. The charge, however, is about the equivalent of $1.00 U.S., so the use is restricted to
middle- and upper-class people. The best swimming pool, however,
is found about five miles out of town on the road to San Miguel de
Allende. It is called "Balneario Lara" and is a newly constructed rec-
reational area. Completely surrounded by a tall, brick wall, the *balneario* has large grassy areas with tables for lunching. There also is a
refreshment bar, a handball court, and a large pool. The admission
charge is the equivalent of $1.00 U.S., a socially restrictive price. The
balneario is very clean and well kept. For people who can pay the fee,
it is a lovely place for an outing.

Poor people seldom go swimming. Few of them know how to
swim, and even fewer have swimsuits. If they go swimming at all, it
is in an irrigation ditch, or they wade a little with their pantlegs
rolled up at the irrigation lake.

G. Children's Games

Children find their own ways to entertain themselves. Among their
pursuits are many universal children's games, such as playing jump
rope (*saltar a la cuerda*) and hopscotch (*rayuela*). As children do
everywhere, the children of Altagracia invent rhymes to accompany
their games. The following nonsensical, rhythmical rhyme often ac-
companies jumping rope: "*Bate, bate, chocolate, con harina y to-
mate*" (Beat it, beat it, chocolate with flour and tomato).

Common throughout Mexico is the children's game *La víbora de la
mar* (The Snake from the Sea). This game is similar to the game of
"London Bridge." This game is played by a group of children while
they sing a song. The words of the song suggest what will happen in
the game. The first verse, for example, is as follows:

A la víbora, víbora de la mar,
por aquí pueden pasar.
El de adelante corre mucho
y el de atrás se quedará.

The snake, the snake from the sea,
through here you can pass.
The one in front runs a lot
and the one behind stays behind.

To play this game, two children join hands and raise them up, forming a bridge under which the other children will pass. The children who have joined hands then lower them to trap another child in their arms at the time indicated by the song.

Campanitas de oro
déjenme pasar,
con todos mis hijos
menos el de atrás, trás, trás.

Little bells of gold
let me pass,
with all my children
except the one at the end, end, end.

The focus of the song is not on the children who form the bridge but on the line of children who form a snake that moves and coils up. Before each game, the two children who will be the bridge choose a secret identity. One might be, for example, the "orange" and the other, the "apple." When one of the other children is caught between their arms, they ask him, "Who will you go with, apple or orange?" The child chooses and then stands behind the one chosen and grasping him or her at the waist. All of the remaining children then get behind either apple or orange to form two snakes. To decide which group is stronger, they do a tug-of-war. The snake that pulls the other over a line drawn in the dirt is the winner of the game. Then two more children are chosen to be the bridge and the game begins again.

Recently, the López family celebrated the eleventh birthday of Irene with a large party. Along with members of the family, friends from the neighborhood and school were invited. The children first played "La víbora de la mar," and then went on to the traditional birthday *piñata*. The *piñata* is a papier-mâché animal, decorated in bright colors. In this case, it was a two-foot high bull, complete with horns. The *piñata* was filled with about a pound of candy and then suspended from a beam by a strong cord or rope. The children took turns trying to hit it with a long stick. To make it more difficult, the older children were blindfolded and turned around several times to disorient them. Then the *piñata* was swung back and forth as each child tried to break it. Finally, one of them broke it, spilling the candy on the patio floor. All the children scrambled to get some, except for Irene, who suddenly decided that perhaps she was too old to play such silly children's games.

♜♙♙♜ 9. ♙♜♙

Meals and Foods

A. Breakfast

Mealtimes and foods are quite different from those in the United States. Breakfast (*el desayuno*) is not typically a family meal. The different members of the family get up between six and seven in the morning and get ready for the day. Before they go to the dining room or the kitchen to eat breakfast, they get dressed to go to work or to school. It would be very unusual to see Mexicans at the breakfast table in pajamas and slippers. Since they all have different schedules, often each member of the family eats breakfast alone.

Breakfast, however, is a very light meal. Usually it consists of a roll or a piece of toast and something to drink, such as coffee, orange juice, or hot chocolate. Children might have a glass of milk to drink.

Poor people seldom can afford milk or fruit juice for breakfast, but bread is cheap and readily available. Vendors go through the poor neighborhoods in the mornings carrying large baskets of bread on their head. Tortillas also are very cheap. Breakfast, then, is likely to consist of some inexpensive tea, maybe even an herb from the market, and bread or tortillas.

B. *El Almuerzo*

About three or four hours after breakfast, most people begin to feel a little bit hungry. After all, breakfast is very light. Around ten or eleven in the morning, they have a snack (*el antojito*). They may have a soft drink (*el refresco*), some cookies (*las galletas*), a doughnut (*la*

73

A food stand in the market

dona), or some fruit. Working men may eat something more substantial, such as eggs and bread. Mexicans refer to this meal as lunch, *el almuerzo.*

C. Lunch

Mexicans call the large meal of the day *la comida* (the meal), which is eaten between two and three in the afternoon. In Altagracia, all the stores and offices close at two, and all the employees and customers go home to have their rather large lunch. Doña Elvira, who is well-known for her culinary skills, often invites friends and family to lunch. Since her children have married and left home, she has never been able to cook only for herself and don Ramón. So even if unexpected guests arrive, there is always plenty of food for everyone.

The *comida* is a family meal, and the entire family is expected to be there unless there is some compelling reason to be absent. This, the largest meal of the day, is usually eaten in the dining room. In middle- and upper-class homes, the *comida* consists of a soup, a salad, a main dish, and dessert. The salad might be a fruit salad in summer, and sometimes has cactus tips (*las tunas*) in it. The main dish is usually a traditional Mexican dish, such as *enchiladas* (a round *tortilla* dipped in sauce and filled with chicken, beef, or pork and covered with sauce and cheese and then rolled), *tamales* (cornmeal-covered chicken, peppers, and sauce wrapped in dried corn husks and steamed), *tacos* (a folded *tortilla* filled with chopped meat, to-matoes, sour cream, and sauce), or some type of pork or beef. People in Altagracia seldom eat fish. The meal may be accompanied by delicious bread rolls (los *bolillos*) or by flour *tortillas* (like a corn flour pancake, but rolled very thin). The *tortillas* are wrapped in a cloth to keep them warm and put in a small, covered basket. The *tortillas* are bought fresh each day from the neighborhood *tortilla* store (*la tortillería*) and brought home wrapped in a cloth inside the same basket from which they are served. Mexicans take a *tortilla* out of the basket, put a spoonful of hot sauce on it, roll it up and eat it along with their meal. They often put generous amounts of hot sauce on most of their food. The typical desserts are a custard dish called *flan* or some fruit and cheese. Many Mexicans also have a glass of wine along with their meal, although children do not.

For poor families, the *comida* is much simpler fare. The staple items in their diet are *tortillas*, refried beans (*frijoles refritos*), rice, hot chili sauce (*salsa picante*), bread, and eggs. About twenty basic food items are subsidized by the government under an economic plan called *el pacto económico* (the economic pact). This government action helps keep prices low for items such as bread, milk, sugar, and oil, which are eaten sparingly. Many poor people suffer from a diet low in calories; they simply don't get enough to eat. Poor working men sometimes have nothing to eat for lunch but plain *tortillas* and hot sauce.

In the summer, fruits and vegetables are inexpensive. Nevertheless, poor people seldom eat meat, and fruits and vegetables in the winter are priced beyond their ability to pay. They occasionally have a little chicken, and the market sells the less desirable cuts of meat, such as the feet and head of pigs, at cheaper prices. The meat offered for sale at street markets sometimes looks so bad that even the hungriest person won't buy it.

Middle-class families are very careful about their table manners. They rest their wrists lightly on the table and never put their left hand in their lap the way people do in the United States. There is a good deal of animated family conversation at these meals. Again, people are expected to be dressed in their street clothes, that is, they dress as if they were going to a restaurant. No one would ever come to the table barefoot or without a shirt on. Shorts are not worn, since they are appropriate only for going to the park or the tennis court.

If the trip back to work is not too long, there may be time for a brief nap or *siesta* after the meal, usually lasting twenty or thirty minutes.

Then it is time to return to work. The stores and offices all reopen at four in the afternoon and remain open until eight at night.

D. Dinner

The evening meal is called *la cena*. People come home from work as soon after eight o'clock as they can, and the *cena* is ready when everyone gets home, usually between 8:30 and 9:30 in the evening. This is also a family meal, and a great effort is made to see that everyone is there. This is a smaller meal than the *comida* but not as small as the *desayuno*. A typical *cena* will have a drink of some kind, such as coffee; cheese; bread; wine or juice; a soup; a smaller main dish; and some dessert.

Because it is difficult to go right to sleep with a full stomach, bedtime comes late. Most people will not go to bed until 11:30 or midnight. In the summer when the children are not in school, they stay up even later. It is not unusual to see small children up at 11:30 or midnight. The nights are very pleasant, and the children can have a nap the next day during the *siesta*.

E. Good Manners and Etiquette

The middle class in Altagracia is anxious to show its prestige and well-being by imitating as much as possible the manners of the upper class. In contrast with the elasticity of manners of the middle class in the U.S., Mexican social interaction offers more elaboration, detail, and rigidity. Greetings are effusive between friends and ceremonial with visitors or distinguished persons. Friends who meet in the street embrace, slapping each other on the back, and women often kiss each other on both cheeks in between exclamations of surprise and happiness. A visitor is not permitted to pay the bill in a café or restaurant even if the host cannot afford to pay the whole thing.

It is considered a social mistake to wear inappropriate clothing. You look bad by wearing the wrong thing, such as no coat and tie for men in a nice restaurant, or by not observing mourning by wearing black for a whole year if a close family member has died. It also is a serious social failing to appear drunk in public.

Courtesy and formality are the rule among families and friends. When Irene López's friends come over to play with her, they always go first to her parents and greet them before going to Irene's room.

Likewise, they always go to Irene's parents to say goodbye before they leave.

Recently, Laura Michaels, a high school student in California and daughter of old friends of Ramón Cabreras, came to stay with Ramón's family in Altagracia for a few weeks to improve her Spanish. She was careful to observe Mexican customs during her stay to avoid shocking or offending Ramón, his wife, and his children. For example, she never walked around the house barefoot because this is considered not only rude, but also bad for your health. She never put her feet up on the furniture, a habit also seen as rude and unattractive. In Mexico, the sight of dirty feet is considered repulsive. Laura also avoided walking around the house partially dressed and never came to the table in her nightclothes. And, out of consideration for her hosts, she turned on lights and appliances only when necessary, since electricity is more expensive in Mexico.

In her interactions with the Cabreras family and the others she met in Altagracia, Laura was mindful of Mexican rules of courtesy. She never wore shorts or a halter downtown. She always said good morning or good afternoon to the family members who were home when she came into the house and when she left the house, she said goodbye to the family members present and told Mrs. Cabreras when she expected to return. Whenever Laura brought friends home with her, she introduced them to the family, since to fail to do this would be to appear badly brought up. Finally, she kept her bedroom open and tidy. In Mexico, the entire house is open to friends and relatives who visit. Since doors are always kept open, it is a bad reflection on the lady of the house for visitors to see a messy room.

Laura had a wonderful stay in Altagracia and returned to California with her Spanish much improved. The Cabreras family also enjoyed her visit and they have invited her to come back as often as she likes.

⌂⌂⌂ 10. ⌂⌂⌂

Traveling

A. Hotels

There is a wide variety of hotels in Altagracia. The best hotel is the "Hotel del Virrey," which faces the square on Aldama Street. It is a beautiful, old colonial mansion, whose central patio has been converted into an attractive dining room. The hallways for the second and third floors open onto the patio. The "Hotel del Virrey" offers swimming and tennis, and also sponsors programs of folk dances and folk singing. Programs take place in the restaurant one or two nights a week in the large central patio. You can enjoy the program along with your meal, with a charge being added for the program, or you can sit on the folding chairs that are put up for people who come only for the program.

At the "Hotel del Virrey," the front desk (*la recepción*) handles all requests for lodging (*el alojamiento*), takes care of reservations (*las reservaciones*), and registers guests (*registrar a los huéspedes*). There are rooms (*las habitaciones*) available with a private bathroom (*el baño privado*) and a tub (*la tina*) and shower (*la regadera*). The bill (*la cuenta*) can be paid at the front desk in cash (*en efectivo*) or with a credit card (*la tarjeta de crédito*). The five months of January, February, July, August, and September are busy travel months in this region of Mexico, and accommodations are often difficult to secure. The prices range from the equivalent of $25.00 to $40.00 U.S. per day.

An inexpensive hotel is the "Hotel Central" on South Juárez Street. It is plain and simple, but it is clean. It has ten rooms, and only half of them have a private bath. The other rooms must use a common bathroom at the end of the hallway.

79

A restaurant with an outdoor dining area

There are also several boardinghouses. The "Casa Rosa" on North Aldama is a good choice. It is a large, old home. The entrance is through a covered driveway which opens onto a large patio where guests eat in good weather. The five rooms all face the patio. Although there are a number of tables in the dining area, the guests often prefer to sit together to enjoy one another's company. The charge for the room includes two meals. The price for one person is the equivalent of $10.00 to $12.00 U.S. a day. Credit cards are not accepted.

On South Núñez Street, near the bullring, there is a very inexpensive hotel, the "Hotel Hidalgo." There are no private baths, the rooms are small and dark, and there is annoying street noise. The inexpensive prices, $2.00 to $3.00 U.S. a day, make this a popular place for students and others who are traveling on a tight budget.

B. Restaurants

There are several good restaurants in Altagracia. The restaurant in the "Hotel del Virrey" is called "El Jardín (The Garden). The patio where this restaurant is located is adorned with many tropical and semitropical potted plants, including bamboo, ferns, spider plants,

RESTAURANTE EL JARDÍN
MENÚ
A LA CARTA

ENSALADAS Y SOPAS (salads and soups)
Ensalada mixta (tossed salad)
Ensalada de lechuga (lettuce salad)
Ensalada de frutas (fruit salad)

Cóctel de camarones (shrimp cocktail)

Aguacate a la vinagreta (avocado in vinegar)

Sopa de cebolla (onion soup)
Crema de champiñones (cream of mushroom soup)

HUEVOS (eggs)
Huevos rancheros (ranch-style omelet)
Huevos tibios, fritos o revueltos (Softboiled, fried, or scrambled eggs)
Omelete al gusto (your choice of omelet)

CARNES (meats)
Pollo frito (fried chicken)
Pollo asado (roast chicken)

Lomo de res (prime rib)
Puntas de filete (beef tenderloin tips)
Chuletas de cerdo (pork chops)
Pierna de cordero (leg of lamb)

PESCADO (fish)
Filete de atún (tuna steak)

LEGUMBRES (Vegetables)
Papas fritas (French-fried potatoes)
Frijoles (beans)
Garbanzos (chickpeas)
Zanahorias (carrots)

BEBIDAS (beverages)
Vino tinto (red wine)
Vino blanco (white wine)
Cerveza (beer)
Té (tea)
Café (coffee)

POSTRES (desserts)
Flan (custard)
Helado de chocolate (chocolate ice cream)
Helado de vainilla (vanilla ice cream)
Pastel de coco (coconut pie)

FRUTAS (Fruit)
Uvas (grapes)
Sandía (watermelon)
Piña (pineapple)
Toronja (grapefruit)
Durazno (peach)

palm trees, and bougainvillea. Following is a typical menu from this fairly expensive restaurant.

The waiter, wearing black pants and a white jacket, takes the order (*el pedido*). He then brings a basket with fresh bread and a dish with butter and then places the table settings (*los cubiertos*) on the table. He also will bring the beverages. The customers can enjoy the bread while waiting for their meal.

Typical soups are creamed corn, chicken broth and noodles, and onion. Salads include a tossed salad (*la ensalada mixta*) or a fruit salad. Among the main dishes, favorites include various forms of chicken, pork chops, lamb chops, steaks, breaded veal, rice dishes, and numerous Mexican dishes—enchiladas, tacos, and tamales.

When the meal is finished, the waiter will not bring the bill (*la cuenta*) until the customers ask for it. People like to stay and talk while they enjoy a cup of coffee.

The restaurant, "La Cartuja," located on the west side of the square, has tables in front that extend up to the sidewalk. This is a very popular place in the evenings. It allows people to sit and have a cup of coffee or a soft drink, chat with friends, and watch all the people walk by. The tables are usually filled in the evenings and on weekends.

The "Café Colón" on Juárez Street is a family-oriented restaurant. At this restaurant most of the items on the menu are for complete meals, such as *enchiladas suizas*. Besides the *enchiladas*, the meal includes rice and refried beans and a beverage.

C. The Travel Agency

In the front of the "Hotel del Virrey" there is a travel agency, "Viajes Sánchez." The travel agents have a computer that is connected to a national system of hotel and airline reservations. The Mexican government operates two airlines, Mexicana de Aviación and Aeroméxico. These two airlines offer service to all areas of Mexico, as well as to the United States, Canada, and Europe.

The travel agency "Águila Viajes," located on Diezmo Street, is affiliated with American Express. The agency also makes arrangements for transportation to the Mexico City airport in a VW bus, which picks you up at your hotel and takes you right to the airport.

A third travel agency, "Agencia de Viajes Alfredo Pinto," also on Diezmo Street, is next door to the "Farmacia Gómez." This is the only travel agency in town that handles train tickets.

🏠🏠🏠 11. 🏠🏠🏠

The Family

A. The Extended Family

For all of the members of the Ramón and Elvira López family, the family always comes first. The family includes the grandparents, don Ramón (*el abuelo*) and doña Elvira (*la abuela*); several aunts (*las tías*) and uncles (*los tíos*); brothers (*los hermanos*), Rogelio and David; and a sister (*la hermana*), Gracia. Also included in the family are grandchildren, nephews and nieces, a brother-in-law and sisters-in-law, and even godparents (*los padrinos*).

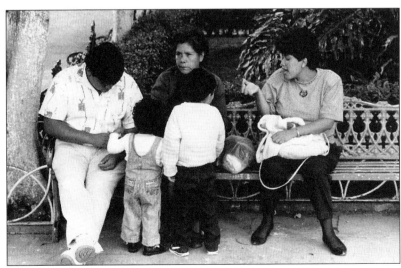

A family in the square

The godparent relationship is taken very seriously. As is the custom, when the good friends of the family, Marcos and Isabel Hernández, became godparents of the oldest son Rogelio, the parents and the godparents changed the way they spoke to each other. From that point on, they have used only the more formal *usted* for "you." This is an indication of the respect they feel for each other. The father and the godfather call one another *compadre* (co-father), while the mother and the godmother call each other *comadre* (co-mother). During the life of the godchild, the godparents will do what they can to help. If something ever happened to the parents, they would not hesitate to take their godchild into their own home and raise him or her as their own.

The importance of the extended family is seen in the Hispanic system of surnames. During the first few days after his birth, Rogelio was baptized and given a name. He was given the first name (*el nombre de bautismo*) of Rogelio and two surnames. The first surname (*el apellido paterno*) is the surname of his father, López. The second surname (*el apellido materno*) is the maiden name of his mother, Martín. See below how this works.

Father			Mother			
Ramón	López	Pérez	Elvira	Martín	Madero	de López
(1)	(2)	(3)	(1)	(2)	(3)	

Child		
Rogelio	López	Martín
(1)	(2)	(3)

The first number (1) indicates the baptismal name, the second number (2) indicates the paternal surname, and the third number (3) indicates the maternal surname. When a woman marries, she keeps all her maiden names and adds *de* plus the husband's paternal surname. By means of this surname system, you are able to determine the family relationships on both sides of the family. When you ask for someone, you use either the first surname alone or both surnames. For example, you would refer to the father as Sr. López or Sr. López Pérez. The mother would be referred to as Sra. de López.

The son, Rogelio, his wife Teresa, and their children Tomás and Irene used to live with Ramón and Elvira in their large, two-story home. This means that, at one time, three generations lived in the grandparent's house, but not just for economic reasons. They like to be surrounded by family. It also means that there is never a need for a babysitter, since there will always be someone at home who can watch the children.

The family remains solid, as an institution that gives strength and stability to Altagracia and the nation. It is one reason why the drastic economic problems that Mexico has experienced in recent years have not produced greater social turmoil. Thousands of people in Altagracia work in small businesses that belong to families. Typically, these businesses are shops (*tiendas*), restaurants, garages, or stands (*puestos*) in the market or in the street. The López family owns a garage called "Mecánica López e Hijos." This automobile repair business was started by grandfather López many years ago. Today, Rogelio and David work in the garage with their father. Their family business enjoys a good reputation, and they have many customers.

The family offers a support system for young (*jóvenes*) and old (*mayores*), orphans and the elderly (*ancianos*), and even visiting relatives. All of these people enjoy security in housing and food, and they often work in family businesses. If work in a family business is not available, then family members help each other find work in shops, garages, large homes, or on nearby farms.

The extended family is even more important for the poor. The poor look for jobs for their relatives at the same place where they are employed. As a result, the maid, the gardener, and the chauffeur of a rich family are often related. There are several poor families from Altagracia who have a number of relatives living in the United States. It starts with one person who goes and finds a job. Then another goes and joins him, and in four or five years there may be seven or eight members of the same extended family living together in the U.S.

B. Frequent Gatherings

Within the family group there is an active social life. Even distant relatives gather frequently for baptisms (*bautismos*), weddings (*casamientos*), anniversaries, burials (*entierros*), and birthdays (*cumpleaños*). These celebrations include all members of the family— even the little children. Next Saturday, for example, the López family will be celebrating the birthday of grandmother López. Sometimes they get together in a caravan of cars and travel out of town a few miles for a picnic. On other occasions, they all gather in the house of the grandparents or the house of an uncle for the celebration. By having frequent family gatherings, all become accustomed to social situations with people of different age groups. The children learn to behave properly around adults, and adults never become too old to be near the little ones.

The members of the López family feel more secure (*seguros*) and comfortable (*cómodos*) when they are surrounded by family. The family continues being the most basic and important institution of Altagracia and Mexico.

C. Male-Female Roles

The man is the head of the household in Altagracia. He is shown respect and the children obey him without question when he is home. Unfortunately, economic and social factors require that most men spend a great deal of time away from home. Many middle-class men have two jobs, while those who have their own business, such as the López brothers, spend long days at their work. Rogelio and David López often spend nine or ten hours a day at their car repair shop. However, they always make a great effort to be home for the afternoon meal. There they preside over the family and lead the conversation. The women members of the family defer to the male members, letting them express their opinions first and waiting on them attentively. When Grandfather López or his son Gregorio want something at home, such as a drink of water, the female family members hurry to fulfill their request. After dinner, no one expects that the male members of the family will lend a hand to clear the table, to wash the dishes or to sweep the floor. Those tasks are not considered "man's work." The responsibility of the man is to provide for the family financially and to oversee, usually from a distance, the well-being and security of the house and family and the development of the children.

Most middle-class fathers openly show affection toward their children. It is a common sight to see young fathers playing with their babies, carrying their young sons as the family strolls in the square, or walking through the streets holding more than one child by the hand. The children are well dressed for these strolls—the boys in long pants, a nice shirt, and leather shoes, and the girls in frilly dresses and white shoes. The fathers are very proud of their families.

In many ways, the apparent pattern of male dominance is just an image that men try to keep intact. In fact, Mexican women have much more power and authority than it would seem at first glance. Many women actually run the financial affairs of the family, since many men turn their money over to their wives. In this way the wife has some flexibility in how the money is actually spent. Because the father is generally absent from home many hours every day, most of the burden of raising and training the children falls on the mother. Most women take an active part in making family decisions. Contrary to the old stereotyped portrayals, most Mexican women are not weak and totally submissive. Many are very strong individuals. Nevertheless, at home the mother and other female members of the family still make the father and brothers feel "superior" by waiting on them and by showing deference to them. For example, regardless of how much they may disagree, Teresa López and the other women from the López family will never embarrass the male members of the family by challenging their authority in front of others or by speaking badly of them in public. In private, however, there is usually a lively exchange of opinions.

Today many women work outside the home, and some from Altagracia have gone to universities in larger cities and have a profession. A good example is Marta Ochoa. She graduated from the State University at Guanajuato with a degree in law. For several years she held an administrative position at a large bank. Now, however, she runs two businesses. One is a private accounting firm and the other is a gift shop in an old mansion near the main plaza. The shop, which has been in her family for generations, features paintings, furniture, and decorative items. Both businesses have been fairly successful and seem to be weathering the nation's economic storms.

D. The *Piropo*

The *piropo* is a popular custom in which men show their appreciation of feminine beauty, grace, and elegance by offering a verbal "flower" to an attractive woman as she passes by on the street. Sometimes the custom is called "throwing flowers" (*echando flores*). It is somewhat similar to the way construction workers whistle at or make comments to women in the United States, but it is much more widespread. In the best of situations, especially in the nicer neighborhoods and the better downtown areas, the *piropo* can be an elegant expression of beauty and grace. Many Latin men see it as a verbal homage to the beauty or the grace of the woman who passes by and also as an example of their own manly wit and charm. Usually women simply continue walking without offering any response. The man doesn't expect any answer.

In poorer neighborhoods and in run-down areas of town, especially at night, the *piropo* can sometimes turn ugly and become crude. The following are samples of *piropos*. The first are simple greetings that are said as men pass by a woman walking toward them. Note that in Spanish when people pass each other in the street they say "Good-bye" rather than "Hello."

¡Adiós, morena!	Hi, brunette!
¡Adiós, rubia!	Hi, blondie!
¡Adiós, linda!	Hi, good-looking!
¡Adiós, preciosa!	Hi, precious!
¡Adiós, simpática!	Hi, sweetie!
¡Adiós, mamacita!	Hi, momma!
¡Adiós, chula!	Hi, cutie!

Men and older boys who are standing on a corner or outside a café will often say a longer piropo, such as the following:

"Eres una flor hermosa y fragante."
(You are a beautiful and fragrant flower.)

"Bendita sea la madre que te parió."
(Blessed be the mother who bore you.)

"Eres una Santa Bárbara. Santa por delante, y bárbara por detrás."
(You are a Saint Barbara. Saintly from the front, and terrific from the back. [This is a play on words. *Bárbara* is both a name and a familiar expression, meaning "splendid" or "terrific."])

"Ay, qué curvas, y yo sin frenos."
(Oh what curves, and me without brakes.)

"Adiós chaparrita, cuerpo de uva."
(Hello, shortie, with a body like a grape. [The idea here is one of well developed and ripe.])

"Qué bonitos ojos."
(What a beautiful eyes.)

ᏮᎥᎣᎧᏬ 12. ᎧᎧᏬ

Religion

The Mexican constitution of 1917, which was patterned after the liberal constitution of Benito Juárez in 1857, reduced the Church to a civil organization. According to this constitution, which is still the basic law of the land, heavy restrictions applied to the Church. The constitution prohibited worship outside church buildings, such as processions. All monasteries and convents were closed, and religious orders and vows were outlawed. All church buildings belonged to the government and were used at the discretion of the government. Priests and ministers became members of a civil profession, and as such were regulated by the government. Only native-born Mexicans could be priests or ministers. Members of the clergy were forbidden in public or private meetings to criticize the laws of the nation or its public officials. The clergy could not vote, hold public office, or assemble for political purposes. Political parties bearing religious names, such as Christian Democrats, were forbidden. All elementary education, public and private, had to be nonreligious. Those who violated the religious restrictions were denied a trial by jury.

These constitutional restrictions were so harsh that they have never been completely enforced. From time to time there is a crackdown by the government, but many of the provisions are seldom enforced. For example, today there are occasional processions, sometimes with hundreds of people, through the streets of Altagracia. When the Pope came to Mexico in 1978, and again in 1990, his every action was technically a violation of the constitution. He wore his robes in public, participated in huge processions, and celebrated large outdoor masses. Yet no one even considered arresting him, for his reception

A religious procession leaves the church

was warm, enthusiastic, and full of hope. Clearly, the wishes of the people, not the constitution, ruled the day.

Nevertheless, in Altagracia, the priests take off their religious robes before leaving the church, and they carry them under their arms as they walk through the streets. Before knocking on the door of a house where they are going to visit, they put on their religious robes over their street clothes as they stand at the entrance.

Most Mexican politicians publicly flaunt their independence from the Church. It is not unusual for a politician to wait outside the church while his son or daughter gets married inside. For example, Altagracia's mayor, Alejandro Palacios, stood outside the church while his daughter was being married inside. Nevertheless, when she and her new husband emerged, Alejandro embraced her, with tears in his eyes.

In spite of these restrictions and conflicts, Mexico is a very religious country. Religion plays an important part in the life of everyone in Altagracia—whether they are religious or not. Doña Elvira López is very devout. She attends mass several mornings a week. She also reminds the children (including her adult sons) of their religious obligations.

Names are nearly always religious in origin; some families will only choose names that appear in the Bible for children.

A. The Saint's Day

Nearly everyone's name is also the name of a saint, and every saint has a celebration day on the Catholic calendar when the saint is to be honored. People who have the name of that saint celebrate their saint's day, which is like having another birthday. The saint's day for Tomás López is December 21, and the day for his sister Irene is April 24. As children, they look forward to the special desserts and presents they receive on their special days.

Stores even plan their advertising around the saints' days coming up each month so people can remember to buy a gift for friends.

B. Everyday Influence

People's everyday lives are influenced by religion. In most places in town, the church bells wake up light sleepers every morning. The bells can be heard at other times of day, too. Many homes have a niche by the front door that contains a statue of Jesus or of Jesus' heart. In the living room, there might be a cross on the wall or a statue of a saint on a table, and in many bedrooms there are crosses and statues. Religious artifacts, such as crosses or rosaries, can be seen on tables. It is not unusual to see a burning candle under a picture of the Virgin Mary.

Celebrating Corpus Cristi Day

Many everyday expressions have a religious origin. For example, an expression of surprise, anger, or alarm is *Dios mío* (my God), *Jesús* (Jesus), and a person agreeing to any appointment may add *si Dios quiere* (if God wants it). Many people, such as athletes, especially those who are superstitious or religious, cross themselves in a moment of danger or difficulty.

C. Holidays and Processions

Many religious holidays are also city, state, or national holidays, such as carnival (Lent), Easter, and Christmas. Often there are large processions or parades witnessed by hundreds of people. Most cities also have a patron saint, and on that saint's day, the community holds a large celebration, sometimes lasting for several days.

An example of one of the many popular religious celebrations is May 15, the Patronal Feast of San Isidro, when animals and seeds are blessed. Animals are washed, brushed, combed, and colorfully adorned. When the church bells ring, a procession of all the animals is formed to pass by the church for blessing. The priest, dressed in his vestments, stands outside the church and is accompanied by acolytes who bear candles and holy water. The town band leads the procession and groups of young and teenaged girls, dressed in regional costumes, pass by on carts or on trucks. At the heart of the celebration come the hardworking oxen, yoked in pairs and adorned with necklaces of corn cobs, ribbons, and flowers for the occasion. They all march by the priest and are blessed, and afterwards there is a special mass. This feast should not be confused with the January 17 Feast of San Antonio when domestic animals and household pets are taken to church to be blessed. Last year, Tomás and Irene took their pet canary. They took turns carrying the cage, but both held it while the canary was being blessed.

Other religious holidays include the first Friday in March. This is the religious ceremony for the Lord of the Conquest. To celebrate, there are special masses, folk dances, and a fireworks display. Two weeks before Easter, there is the procession of the Lord of the Column. The statue of the *Señor* is paraded from the town of Atotonilco, in stages, to a local church, where the people sing amid a profusion of flowers.

D. Competition from Protestants

Today in Altagracia, the Catholic Church has competition from Protestants. Most have come from the United States, and some of them have made great strides. The most popular of these Protestant churches are the Evangelical or Pentecostal sects. They are characterized by divine healing, speaking in tongues, and emotional fervor. On the other hand, businessmen have been attracted to the more traditional Protestant groups, such as the Lutherans or the Methodists, which they join at the same time as they join the Rotary Club. They are small groups in Altagracia. The businessmen often see these religions as a way to leave their traditional molds and to modernize themselves. Other religions that have had success in Altagracia are the Seventh-Day Adventists and the Mormons. In a new section of town, the Mormons have built a large new chapel and, for the young people, an outdoor basketball court. Mormon missionaries also work in town.

The newer Protestant churches are usually politically conservative, leaving them open to charges by leftist politicians that they are agents of the CIA or representatives of the United States government. Since there are few leftists in Altagracia who are politically active, it isn't much of a problem for the Protestants. The Protestants do skirt the constitutional question, however, since few of their missionaries or ministers are Mexican citizens. They usually come into Mexico with student or tourist visas.

Ⓐ 13. Ⓑ

Education

The Mexican educational system has followed European models. A centralized Ministry of Education plans the educational programs for the entire nation. There is no local school board or any other local control. In theory, under the centralized system, all the children in a particular grade should be studying the same lesson on a given day.

Uniform textbooks and curricula are prepared at the national level, which is advantageous because well-known experts in the field write the materials that are provided free to the schools, making it possible for more children to have books. The system has the disad-

Schoolboys ready for a celebration

vantage that most of the textbooks in the social sciences and history are leftist in orientation, and there is little that people who hold different views can do about it.

All teachers are hired nationally under a single salary schedule, although sometimes bonuses are offered for teaching in remote areas. Most teachers prefer to teach in the large cities; therefore, it is sometimes difficult to find qualified teachers to teach in Altagracia. Because of this difficulty and the low wages, many of the teachers are very young and inexperienced. When the government has financial problems, it is not unusual for it to fall behind in paying teachers. A lack of funds also means some of the school buildings are very old and not well maintained. Throughout the country, there is a shortage of teachers. Some schools in Altagracia have as many as 45 students in a single class, a common national problem.

A. Nursery School

Children begin nursery school (*el Kinder*) at age five. The government provides some nursery schools, but there are not enough to satisfy the demand. Many middle-class families prefer to send their children to private nursery schools. These half-day schools are intended to familiarize students with the school environment. Children learn to relate to other children and begin to learn to use pencils and crayons. They also learn the basic colors and numbers.

B. Primary School

Children begin primary school (*la escuela primaria*) at age six, and undergo a six-year basic educational program. All primary school students wear a uniform. The boys wear a blue jacket and blue pants, while the girls wear either a similar blue jacket and skirt or a one-piece blue dress, and blue knee-length socks.

Irene López is in the fifth year, or fifth grade, at school and for the most part, she enjoys wearing the blue uniform. However, she is beginning to wonder why she can't dress like the rock stars that she sees on television.

The subjects Irene and other public school students study are the same as in most countries—namely, reading, writing, and arithmetic, along with social studies and history. Traditional learning methods of recitation and memorization are used in these schools,

Waiting outside a primary school

partly because of tradition and partly because of the large classes. Children show what they have learned by repeating memorized lessons in chorus. Numerous rhythms are used to aid pronunciation drills. For example, a common one for teaching the sound of the Spanish double *r*, which is difficult for many children, is as follows:

> Erre con erre cigarro.
> Erre con erre barril.
> Rápido corren los carros
> Los carros del ferrocarril.

The primary school operates a daily two-session program. One group comes in at seven in the morning and remains until one o'clock. Another group comes in at two in the afternoon, which means they have to eat the *comida* (midday meal) early, and they remain until nine at night.

C. High School

The high school is called a *colegio* and is a three-year program, beginning at age twelve. The high school curriculum is divided into two three-year cycles. The first three years constitute the basic cycle, and consist of general studies in history, math, foreign languages, social studies, geography, and Spanish language and literature. Everyone takes the same classes, and there are no electives.

A partial view of an educational complex

Tomás López is in the first year of the *colegio*. He already knows that he wants to go to the university after leaving high school, so he takes his studies more seriously than many boys his age. Everyone in the family, especially his mother and his grandmother Elvira, encourages him to do well.

Following high school, there is a three-year program at a preparatory school, *la preparatoria*. Students must pass a rigorous examination to be admitted. Some students can't pass the test, and others spend an entire year studying for it. This second three-year cycle constitutes the advanced level and includes courses that are focused on different academic areas. For example, there is the science area for those who intend to major in a science at the university such as math, chemistry, medicine, or engineering. There is a humanities area for those intending to major in such things as language, literature, theater, or art. The social science area is for those who intend to go into law, psychology, or sociology. In this way, students already start the preparatory work for their university majors while they are still in high school. Because they are divided according to interest and knowledge, they are able to accomplish a good deal. The ordinary diploma from the preparatory school is the Bachelor's title or degree (*el bachillerato*). Since only students who are preparing to go to the university attend the preparatory school, the student body is a select and academically talented group.

Students who do not go to high school at all or who only go through the basic cycle can attend other types of schools for vocational or technical training. Training is available in subjects such as business (typing, shorthand, bookkeeping, and computers), beauty school, electronics (TV, radio, and appliance repair), drafting, and mechanics. In these programs, students spend several years of full-time classroom study and undergo a part-time apprenticeship or on-the-job training.

For these reasons, many observers say that the Mexican high school degree is worth more than a diploma from the U.S. Students in the U.S. would need about a year of university or junior college work to be equal to what Mexican students accomplish in the traditional areas of geography, political science, literature, art, history, and oral and written expression, or language arts.

Mexican students have few elective subjects. Maybe they could choose between French or English as a foreign language but not between foreign languages and, say, mass media. Also, competitive sports between schools do not exist.

The system of grading is based on a scale of five to ten. Since the grading is fairly tough, hardly anyone ever receives a ten, which would be equivalent to an A + . Grades of eight and nine correspond to a B or an A − . Grades of six and seven are passing (*aprobado*), while a grade of five is failing (*reprobado*). Not many tests or quizzes are given during the year; however, there are two long written examinations. The midterm (*el intermedio*) is given after half the year,

A typing room at a vocational school

and the final exam (*el examen final*) is given at the end of the year. Attendance and homework assignments are the other factors that help determine a grade. Tomás López is a typical student. He is studying eight subjects (*las materias*). If at the end of the year, he passes six of them and fails two, he will be allowed to continue on to the next level. However, during the next year, he would be required to pass the two failed courses. If he never does pass them, he will not be allowed to graduate. There is also another opportunity to take the exams in the summer before the beginning of the next year. If the student failed three or more courses, then he would have to repeat the entire year. Of course, Tomás usually receives average to above-average grades and does not need to worry about repeating courses.

Since there are usually not enough high schools or preparatory schools, sometimes students cannot enroll in a school right away and must wait for a year. To help alleviate the crowding, the high schools have two sessions daily. The first begins at 7:00 A.M. and goes to 1:30 P.M. The second one begins at 1:30 P.M. and ends at 7:00 P.M. At the Technical High School, the curriculum is more demanding, and the students must attend eight hours a day.

Most teachers are paid by the course (and usually do not receive very much). Therefore, many teachers teach at two or more schools—one in the morning shift and one in the afternoon and sometimes even a third at night.

A sewing room at the vocational school

D. Adult Education

The Educational Complex at the south end of Juárez Street includes a technical school, *el Centro de Capacitación*. This school not only has programs for high school students, but it also offers courses in six areas for adults. The adult education courses are auto mechanics (*mecánica automotriz*), electronics (*electrónica*), secretarial skills (*secretariado*), ceramics and pottery (*cerámica y alfarería*), dressmaking (*confección de ropa*), and weaving (*tejido mecánico de punto*).

These adult education courses run three hours a day for six months and are offered in the daytime and in the evening. The cost (*cuota de inscripción*) is very low, about three times the daily wage of the student. If adult students earn the minimum wage of about $3.50 U.S. a day, the *cuota* would be equal to $10.50 U.S.

There are four levels of sewing classes. The first one deals with simple hand-stitching and an introduction to the sewing machine. The second course deals with clothing for women and children. The third course deals with clothing for men, and the fourth course is high-fashion sewing (*alta costura*). At the end of the fourth course, the school sponsors a fashion show at the "Hotel del Virrey." The mayor and several businessmen usually attend.

The buildings where these classes are held are modern and well equipped. Both students and instructors are proud of this facility. It makes an important contribution to the town and the surrounding area.

Classroom Activities

Introduction and Town Layout

1. Examine a map of Mexico and decide where you think Altagracia might be located.
   a. How far is it from Mexico City and Guadalajara?
   b. What is the capital of the state where it is located, and what is the name of the capital city?

2. What do you think the name Altagracia means? Break it down into *alta* and *gracia* and look them up in a Spanish-English dictionary.

3. Draw a map of your own imaginary town. Think about where in Mexico you would like to place it. Locate the main square and the most important institutions. What would you name the town and the square?

4. List four or five activities that take place in the main square.
   a. What influence does the climate have in determining the kinds of activities?
   b. Where did the ancestors of the residents of Altagracia come from? What kind of town life did they have there?

5. Trace the street map of Altagracia. Then, as you study other sections of the book, locate them on your map.

6. How far from someone do you stand when you talk to that person?

7. Is your city laid out in a grid pattern or a star pattern? Is there a central meeting place?

2. Housing

1. In what ways are Mexican houses different from houses in the United States?
   a. List four or five things that are different about them.
   b. Give three or four reasons why Mexican houses are not like houses in the United States.
   c. Does your house have a patio?

2. Draw a floor plan of a Mexican house. Label the different rooms in Spanish and English.
   a. Will the house need a heating system?
   b. Where will the children play?
   c. How will the family keep cool in the summer?

3. How does the use of the living room in your house compare with the use of *la sala* in a Mexican house?
   a. Where does the Mexican family watch television?
   b. Where does your family watch television?

4. Where does a Mexican family eat their meals? How does this compare with families in the U.S.?

5. Make a list of four or five things that the patio might offer a Mexican family.
   a. How do families in the U.S. carry out these activities?
   b. How does a backyard in the U.S. compare with a patio?
   c. Why do you think the Spanish language doesn't have a word for "yard," as in "front yard"?

6. What are some differences in construction methods and materials between U.S. and Mexican houses?

3. Shops and Shopping

1. Compare where middle-class and poor people buy clothing.
   a. What are some advantages of having your clothing hand-made?
   b. What clothing characterizes poor men and women?

2. Where could people of Altagracia go to buy a gift?
   a. Where do you buy a gift for a baby?

    b. What kinds of items do the shops under the arches at the north end of the square sell?

    c. What kinds of things do vendors sell in the square?

3. Where do people go to buy food items?

    a. Does the market cater only to poor people?

    b. What are some of the social aspects of shopping in the market?

    c. What are typically Mexican food products that are sold in the market?

    d. Make a list of the specialty food stores.

    e. Where would people in the U.S. buy the products that are sold in the Mexican specialty stores?

4. What kinds of things are sold at the street markets? What are the advantages of having a weekly street market in a neighborhood?

5. With a classmate, dramatize a bargaining situation. One of you will be the vendor and the other will be the customer. Decide on the product.

    a. Do you think bargaining is a fair way to establish a price?

    b. What would a Mexican think of a tourist who accepts the first price offered?

    c. Why would a tourist from the U.S. accept the first price?

4. Transportation

1. How do most people in Mexico travel? Why?

2. If someone doesn't have a car, how does he or she get from home to the bus station?

3. What are the advantages and disadvantages of traveling on a first-class bus?

4. What are advantages and disadvantages of traveling on second-class buses?

5. What is a "chicken bus" and why is it called that?

    a. Why would people ride on such a bus?

    b. Can you think of a different way of providing transportation for the people who ride these buses?

6. Draw a picture of a "chicken bus." Label the products carried on the roof.

7. Look at the different bus schedules. What are the choices for traveling to Mexico City?

8. If several bus lines have similar schedules, what would cause a customer to choose one carrier over another?

9. With a classmate, dramatize a situation in which a traveler talks to a ticket agent for a particular carrier about departures to a city. Choose the city and the bus line. Decide on prices in pesos. Reverse roles and role-play another situation.

10. What choices are there to travel by train from Altagracia?

11. List three possible ways of getting from Altagracia to the Mexico City airport.

12. Where would a car owner go to have his or her car lubricated? What does a *servicio completo* include?

13. What are the choices in gasoline? What are the choices in service stations?

14. Compare the shapes and purposes of Mexican road signs with signs in the U.S.

15. What does it mean when a large truck on the highway turns on the right turn signal when the car behind indicates that it wants to pass?

5. Public Services

1. How does a Mexican post office compare with one in the United States?

2. What services are offered at the post office in Altagracia?

3. Why shouldn't you lick stamps?

4. Do you think it is a good idea for the mail carrier to blow a whistle when he leaves a letter?

5. With a classmate, role-play a situation in which one of you is a person wishing to make a long-distance phone call and the

other one is the employee who takes the information and arranges for the call. Decide where to make the call.

6. Why do they use a token rather than money to operate public phones?

7. How do the hours of operation and the services of Mexican banks compare with banks in the U.S.?

8. What is required to cash a traveler's check in Mexico?

9. Why do Mexican banks accept payment for utility bills?

10. Why don't Mexican banks have drive-in windows?

6. Entertainment

1. What are the most popular types of movies? Why?

2. List four different activities that take place in the park.

3. Make a drawing of a park. Label the different areas.
   a. What things would you add?
   b. How would your additions fit in with Mexican culture?

4. Compare the kinds of stores that students in the U.S. visit on their way to and from school with those that the Mexican students visit.

5. Why don't students in the U.S. spend time in cafés?

6. Why don't Mexicans consider bullfighting a sport?
   a. Are there other sports that are violent? Boxing? U.S. football?
   b. With a classmate, write five or six statements in favor of and against bullfighting. Compare your statements with those of others in your class.

7. List four or more similarities and differences between a western rodeo and a Mexican *charreada.*
   a. In what ways have the Mexican ranching and horse industries influenced ranching and horse riding in the U.S.?
   b. List ten words that came from Spanish into English, dealing with the horse and cattle industry.

8. What activities take place in the Art School? What groups benefit from the school?

9. Is there an institution in your community that offers the services that the Art School does?

10. Compare the events sponsored by the Art School with those sponsored by the Theater.

7. The Hospital and Health Care

1. Locate the hospital on the city map. What would be the best route to take from the "Hotel del Virrey" to the hospital?

2. What kinds of health insurance are available for the citizens of Altagracia?

3. Who uses the private clinics?

4. Whom do you call to request an ambulance? What is a second source?

5. Do doctors in your city or town make house calls? Why do you think they do in Altagracia?

6. Why don't more poor people go to medical doctors?

7. What is folk medicine?
   a. Name some examples of nonscientific medicine in the United States (e.g., copper bracelets, health food stores, cancer cures).

8. What is the relationship between "hot foods" and temperature or seasoning?

8. Sports and Recreation

1. Compare the groups who play soccer in the United States with those who play it in Mexico.
   a. Are there soccer leagues for children in your community?
   b. Is soccer a school sport in the high schools of your community?

c. If soccer is the most popular sport in the world, why do you think there are no professional leagues in the United States?

2. What sports in the United States place emphasis on skill with the hands?

3. In view of the use of the feet in U.S. football, do you think its name adequately describes it?

4. Find a book that describes soccer. Draw an outline of the field. How does it compare with a U.S. football field? How do the number of players, their positions, and their functions compare with U.S. football?

5. What is the most popular sport in your area? What is your favorite sport?

6. How does the children's game *La vibora de la mar* compare or contrast with the game "London Bridge"?

9. Meals and Foods

1. How does the Mexican breakfast compare with your breakfast?

2. List three reasons that might explain why Mexicans eat that kind of breakfast.

3. What word do we have in English that might compare to the Mexican early lunch, *el almuerzo*?

4. With a classmate, make lists of the times of eating and the type of food eaten in Mexico and in the United States. One of you should make the list of the times and the foods that your family eats, and the other should make a list of the meals and the foods that the Mexicans eat.

5. What is the largest meal of the day in Altagracia? Describe when it is served, who attends, and what dishes are eaten.

6. What differences are there in the foods eaten by poor people and those eaten by middle-class people in Mexico? in the U.S.?

7. What is the Mexican evening meal called? When is it served? How does it differ from the afternoon meal?

8. With a classmate, discuss the section on manners and etiquette. List four or five manners or customs that are different from those in the United States.
   a. What do you wear when you eat breakfast?
   b. What do you wear around the house?

10. Traveling

1. What services are provided by the "Hotel del Virrey"?

2. What are the busy months for travel in Altagracia?

3. With a classmate, role-play a situation of checking into a hotel. One of you will be the clerk and the other, the customer. Ask about accommodations, prices, and means of payment.

4. Look at the menu from the "Restaurante El Jardín." Write down the items you would like to have for dinner.

5. Use the menu to role-play a situation in which one person is a waiter and two others are customers in the restaurant. Order a meal and pay for it.

6. Find a map of Mexico. Locate on it several areas that you might want to visit.
   a. Make a list of activities that you could do at each place.
   b. What would be the best time to visit these places?
   c. What means of transportation would you use?

7. Using the information obtained in question 6, role-play a situation with a classmate. The classmate will be a travel agent and you will be the traveler. Then reverse roles and act out another situation.

11. The Family

1. What does the word *family* mean in Mexico? Make a list of the relationships that make up a family.

2. Why would godparents be considered part of a family? What is the function of godparents?

3. If we used the Hispanic surname system in the United States, what would your name be? What would the names of your parents be?

4. How does a woman's name change when she gets married?

5. Why aren't babysitters used often in Altagracia?

6. List four or five ways in which a Mexican family functions as a support system.

7. What social events are celebrated by families? What are some advantages of having little children and adults together at social events?

8. Are women completely passive and dominated by men in Altagracia? What evidence is there of power and authority in women?

9. What is a *piropo*? Is there anything like it in the United States?

10. How should a woman react to a *piropo*?

12. Religion

1. List four or five ways in which the constitution of Mexico limits religion.
   a. Why do you think such severe restrictions were applied to religion?
   b. In what ways do priests and nuns have fewer rights than ordinary citizens in Mexico?

2. What religious events take place regularly that are in violation of the constitution?

3. Was the visit of the Pope in keeping with the constitution? Why or why not?

4. What is a person's saint's day?

5. Do you have a name that is the name of a saint? Find a Catholic calendar and see. If you do, when is your saint's day?

6. Make a list of everyday influences of religion.
7. What are some typical religious holidays?
8. How is the Feast of San Isidro celebrated in Mexico?
9. What competition does the Catholic Church have in Altagracia?

13. Education

1. What is the model for education in Mexico?
2. What are some advantages of a centralized educational system?
3. Why is it sometimes difficult to find qualified teachers for the schools in Altagracia?
4. How is the nursery school organized? What children attend?
5. Describe the uniform that children in Altagracia wear to elementary school.
6. Do you think a uniform tends to lessen differences between students, for example, between rich and poor?
7. What are the choices in schedules for elementary school?
8. At what age do students begin high school? Does this seem young to you?
9. How long is the high school program and what subjects are studied?
10. What school do college-bound students attend after high school?
    a. How is this school organized?
    b. What are the advantages of such an organization?
    c. What degree do students receive from this school?
11. What grading system is used?
12. What happens to a person who fails one class in high school?
13. What education or training is available for those who don't want to go to the university?

14. What adult education is available?
    a. Is the cost of these programs within the reach of poor people?
    b. Locate the educational complex on the map.
    c. How do students in the high-fashion sewing class celebrate the end of the year?

NTC SPANISH CULTURAL AND LITERARY TEXTS AND MATERIAL

Contemporary Life and Culture
"En directo" desde España
Cartas de España
Voces de Puerto Rico
The Andean Region

Contemporary Culture—in English
Spain: Its People and Culture
Welcome to Spain
Life in a Spanish Town
Life in a Mexican Town
Spanish Sign Language
Looking at Spain Series

Cross-Cultural Awareness
Encuentros culturales
The Hispanic Way
The Spanish-Speaking World

Legends and History
Leyendas latinoamericanas
Leyendas de Puerto Rico
Leyendas de España
Leyendas mexicanas
Dos aventureros: De Soto y Coronado
Muchas facetas de México
Una mirada a España

Literary Adaptations
Don Quijote de la Mancha
El Cid
La Gitanilla
Tres novelas españolas
Dos novelas picarescas
Tres novelas latinoamericanas
Joyas de lectura
Cuentos de hoy
Lazarillo de Tormes
La Celestina
El Conde Lucanor
El burlador de Sevilla
Fuenteovejuna
Aventuras del ingenioso hidalgo
    Don Quijote de la Mancha

Civilization and Culture
Perspectivas culturales de España
Perspectivas culturales de Hispanoamérica

For further information or a current catalog, write:
National Textbook Company
a division of *NTC Publishing Group*
4255 West Touhy Avenue
Lincolnwood, Illinois 60646-1975 U.S.A.